THE
SNAPSHOT
BOOK

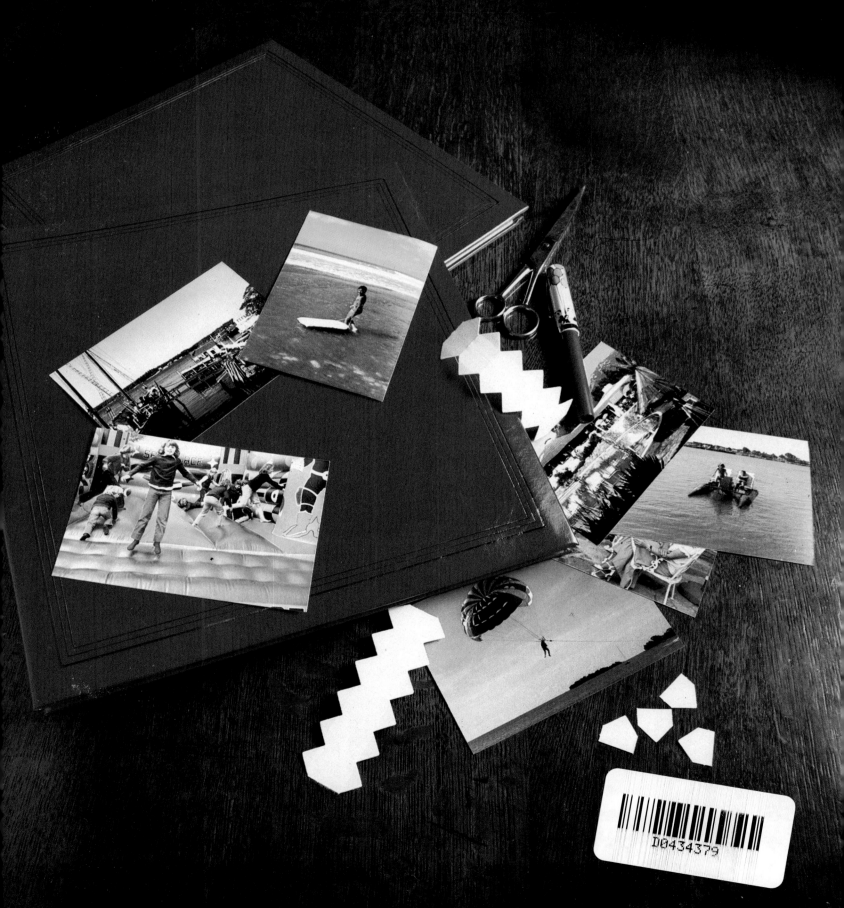

THE SNAPSHOT BOOK

ROGER HICKS

Designed by
PHILIP CLUCAS MSIAD

Produced by
TED SMART and **DAVID GIBBON**

Colour Library Books

CONTENTS

IN PRAISE OF THE SNAPSHOT

A snapshot, like love, is a very private matter. We have all heard the old cry, "I can't think what he sees in her"; and even if we have managed to restrain ourselves from saying it, we must surely have harboured the same thought for the more extraordinary mismatches of our friends.

So it is with snapshots. What is to one person a blurred, fuzzy, indistinct picture of what appears to be a child falling over, is to another a precious record of a daughter's first steps: and what to you is simply a tiresome picture of an Edwardian child standing on one leg is of great value to me, because the child in question was my grandmother in 1907.

For something which is so widely practised, snapshot photography is held in remarkably poor esteem. It is not just the photo-snob, hung about with half a year's salary in the form of cameras and lenses, who says dismissively, "Oh . . . a snapshot," but also the snapshotter himself. "I'm afraid they're not very good," he says, "just snaps."

This dismissive attitude results from a confusion in the minds of most people about the nature of photography. The argument about Photography and Art has raged so long, and so pointlessly, that people tend to forget that photography itself is neutral; you can use it to create a work of art, or a technical record, or just an <u>aide-memoire.</u> To take an analogy, you can use words to write a sonnet, a mathematical textbook, or a shopping list. To say that one is 'better' than another is meaningless: a sonnet is not much use when you need a shopping list (unless you can cast your shopping list into sonnet form), and in the mathematical textbook you are more concerned with clarity of

exposition than with deathless prose. The words are neutral, just as photography is neutral: it is the use to which you put them which gives them value and meaning.

A snapshot is essentially a private photograph. It does not seek to stand alone, to be appreciated for its own sake, like a pictorial photograph; nor does it particularly try to communicate some human predicament, after the fashion of a reportage photograph, though of course it may well do so. Instead, it reminds the photographer, and perhaps a few of his immediate family and friends, or those who were with him of a time or place which he valued highly enough to photograph.

Another thing which distinguishes the snapshot from the photograph with greater pretensions is that the snapshot is usually incidental to some other activity; in other words, the photograph is not the important thing. Contrast that with the small horde of 'serious amateurs' who can be found around any reasonably photogenic spot, especially in a city centre, on a

Childhood days captured on film will yield a rich harvest of memories in years to come. ***Below left:*** *Wind-blown bubbles epitomise the fleeting moment. The shade of an overhanging tree provided the required dark backdrop, whilst the choice of a wide aperture* helped isolate the subject from what would otherwise have been a distracting background. ***Below and facing page:*** *Accustomed to being photographed, many children will ignore the camera, endowing the resultant snapshot with a truly candid quality.*

Yashica Electro 35 GSN. 35mm camera with f1.7 45mm lens,
coupled rangefinder focusing, aperture priority automatic exposure,
shutter 30-1/500, delayed action.

IN PRAISE OF THE SNAPSHOT

Sunday morning. Camera in hand, and often with impatient children in tow (taken for a walk to give their mother some peace in which to prepare the Sunday dinner), they squint through their expensive cameras in a frenzied search for a picture – perhaps even a Picture. To them, the photograph is the thing; to the snapshotter, the subject or activity photographed is the thing, and the photograph is a bonus.

The word 'snapshot' has changed its meaning somewhat over the years. A hundred years and more ago, it was quite a difficult technique: long exposures and bulky cameras made casual picture-taking all but impossible. Then, the 'snapshot' was more like what is now called reportage or photo-journalism: people such as Paul Martin, who was working as late as the 1890s, used concealed or 'detective' cameras to capture candid shots of the world around him. Bear in mind that this was in the days when the more reactionary photographers were still fighting a rearguard action against shutters; exposures of many seconds or even minutes were quite usual, and the old technique of using the lens-cap, or even the photographer's hat, was sufficient. Those masochists who delighted in photographing the interiors of mediaeval churches sometimes measured their exposures in <u>hours,</u> or at least in large fractions of hours.

In the eighteen-eighties, the invention of the rapid dry plate had sparked off a major increase in amateur photography, and in August 1888 George Eastman's celebrated Kodak came out with the famous slogan; 'You press the button, we do the rest.' There was no question of focusing: everything beyond about eight feet was more-or-less sharp. There was no problem about setting other controls either: apart from the winding knob and the shutter release, there weren't any. The Kodak cost $25, with the film in, and once you had shot all 100 of the 2½″-diameter circular pictures the film could hold, you sent it back to Kodak.

Above and right: Unusual characters will lend colour to your holiday snaps and are therefore worth looking out for.
Top: *Local inhabitants will often happily agree to pose for photographs. When taking such shots, ensure that the camera is kept level, and that the subjects are framed well within the area of the viewfinder.*

Kodak Ektralite 400. 110 cartridge load pocket camera, f6.8 24mm lens, fixed focus, weather symbol exposure setting, shutter 1/60-1/250, built-in electronic flash.

Left: Full-length figures in the middle of your picture are fine, but sometimes a better result can be gained by just showing part of your subject off-centre. An overall balance should however be maintained, and here this is achieved by including the brightly coloured balloons, which help relieve the otherwise monotonous background greenery. © Walt Disney Productions. **Below:** A well chosen viewpoint, together with a small aperture ensure that both subject and the attractive background are clearly seen. The dog, complete with lei, provides the humour.

Shows especially mounted for tourists are tailor made for the snapshot photographer; they are colourful and epitomise the spirit of the people and the place. Memories of a friendly people and the gentle sound of their music were captured in the shot **left,** in which a low viewpoint avoided showing too much foreground and used the exotic background to provide mood. **Above:** A low camera angle helped emphasise the whirling dancer by using the sky as a plain background.

9

IN PRAISE OF THE SNAPSHOT

They developed and printed the film, reloaded the camera, and sent the lot back for $10. Admittedly you could only take snapshots in good weather, but now they were within the reach of anyone with the money to buy a camera; and to this day that is one of the main attractions of the snapshot.

In fact, you can take snapshots with just about any camera, as discussed in the next chapter. Any photographer who decries the snapshot, and swears that he never takes them, is either lying or missing out on a major part of photography. I and many of my photographer friends use very expensive cameras in our work, but we do not hesitate to use them for snapshots if that is what we want – in fact, the term 'happy snaps', used in so derogatory a way by certain amateur snobs, is the one we have adopted to describe them. They are snaps, in that we do not devote any great effort to getting them, and they are certainly happy – I for one do not take snapshots when I am miserable.

Below: A long-focus lens was used for this attractive portrait-type snap. This helped to frame just the head in the viewfinder, without moving in too close to the subject. The combination of long lens and wide aperture limits the depth of field, and makes careful focusing essential. In such circumstances it is usual to focus on the eyes or bridge of the nose so that the main facial features remain sharp.

Self-conscious children may be reluctant to pose for a photograph. However, a suggestion that they show off their favourite pet to the camera will invariably make them more amenable. Their happiness and pride will show in the results, and the pictures are likely to be of more interest to them in the future.

What sort of things, then, do we photograph? Very much the same as anyone else. Holidays are an obvious example; children are another; personal occasions, such as weddings, christenings, parties; and public occasions, such as royal weddings, presidential inaugurations, the local floral pageant or carnival, or the Harvest Festival at church. Some things, such as dimly-lit church interiors during the Harvest Festival celebrations, are obviously more difficult to photograph than others, and there are other occasions where an approach using professional equipment and know-how might differ from a simpler approach using a box camera, but to a surprising extent the ground-rules and the basic techniques are the same whether you are using an old Box Brownie which has been lurking at the back of the closet for twenty years, or a Nikon.

The first essential in taking a good snapshot is that we have some idea of what we expect from it: what it is, what we want to

Lubitel 166B. 120 roll-film twin lens reflex.
f4.5 75mm lens, manual exposure,
shutter 1/15-1/250, delayed action.

Left: Fascinated by the antics of some ducks, this unsuspecting group was snapped from behind, to give a pleasing if unconventional family photograph. A familiarity with your camera will enable such shots to be taken without undue thought. *Below left:* Children are best photographed at their own level, even if this means lying down. Long lenses are useful for their frame-filling properties, and a stop-down facility will enable you to accurately determine the depth of focus on single lens reflex cameras. Hair and grass textures are accentuated by strong sunlight almost directly above the subject. *Below:* By focusing the camera on the hamster, because of its relatively small size, equal treatment has been given to both the subjects. The reverse treatment would have spoilt the effect. A fast shutter speed was necessary to freeze any unexpected movement by the animal.

IN PRAISE OF THE SNAPSHOT

do with it, and how other people are likely to respond to it. Here we come back to the essential concept of a snapshot being a private and personal thing.

The extreme example is probably photographs of our children. People who have previously regarded children with an acute lack of interest, possibly even distaste, find when they have one of their own that they provide fascination. This fascination extends to pictures of them. They change at an incredible rate, so that there is a marked difference almost from day to day, and certainly from month to month, and every picture is a personal historic document. Their activities are so novel that when they first crawl, or walk, or even learn to play with their toes, we are captivated. Their first day at kindergarten, at school, at college… the years pass so quickly that we can hardly believe it.

Unfortunately this fascination with our children seldom extends to other people. To be sure, their grandparents will avidly seize upon every picture; and in a few years' time, their fiancés and fiancées will be fascinated to see how their beloved looked so many years ago. Friends with children of a similar age will display more than a passing interest, as may godparents (though equally they may not). But in general, people are not <u>that</u> interested in how your children look. A single photograph is one thing, or even half a dozen pictures shown around the office or whatever every six months or so, but to give someone thirty-six pictures of your pride and joy (and we have seen it done – how often have we seen it done!) is likely to produce the opposite

effect to that intended. Instead of being engrossed in every tiny variation of expression, the hapless victim will flip perfunctorily through the lot, at a loss for words; whereas if he had only been shown one or two pictures, he might have been able to make some intelligent comment. As it is, he will have been thoroughly scared off the subject, and will never enquire after the child again.

The more immediately personal the experience, the less interested other people are likely to be. I have many pictures of my girlfriend (now my wife) taken during her first trip to England. Many of them are rank snapshots; in one, for example, she is standing in an anonymous church doorway. In fact, it is the parish church of St. Denys, in Cornwall, the village where I was born and the church in which I was christened. Certainly, it shows what she looks like, but that is about its only detectable extrinsic merit. Intrinsically, it is a picture which we both value very highly – but one which we would not dream of showing to anyone except our immediate families. Of course, this is even more true of the less flattering views of her. In the George, at Norton St. Philip, there is a tame raven, and I have a picture of Frances on all fours stretching out to stroke its head. Unfortunately, I had a 24mm lens on the camera I was using at the time, and her <u>derriere</u> is closest to the camera. Because of the wide-angle effects described in the next chapter, she looks quite unfairly pear-shaped. We both like the picture, but I would fear for my life if I dared to print it!

With the possible exception of *children, holidays account for the expenditure of more film than any other subject. The novelty of foreign lands and their people should provide inspiration for a wide variety of snapshots. Basically we will photograph what appeals to us, however, it is worth trying to capture, in a series of 'establishing shots', what to us is the essential character of the country. Examples are shown on these pages to demonstrate the value of such snapshots as a means of instant national identification.*

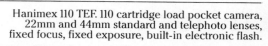

Hanimex 110 TEF. 110 cartridge load pocket camera, 22mm and 44mm standard and telephoto lenses, fixed focus, fixed exposure, built-in electronic flash.

IN PRAISE OF THE SNAPSHOT

At the other end of the scale, shared experiences such as holidays, or records of royal visits or flower pageants, are much more easily appreciated by other people. Even though they did not share your holiday, and may never have been to the place that you photographed, they are still likely to want to see the pictures. They may want to see what the place is like, with a view to going there themselves, or they may simply want to share vicariously in your good fortune. If it is a local event, such as the opening of a new shopping centre or a parade, they may well have their own memories of the event and look to your pictures to confirm or supplement these.

Just as with the pictures of your children, though, it is as well to edit the pictures before you present them. At the very least, pull out the utterly irrelevant pictures which you shot to finish up the roll – the dog, the interior of the kitchen, the experimental shots by candlelight or firelight which didn't quite come off, and so forth – and preferably remove all the duplicate or near-duplicate shots as well as the ones with technical shortcomings. It may mean reducing the number of pictures you show by 50%, or even 90%, but at least the pictures you <u>do</u> show will be worth looking at.

And that brings us onto the last thing about the snapshot: how do you present it? To a large extent this depends on what sort of person you are, but there are a number of alternatives to the usual habit of leaving them in the envelopes in which they

Yashica Autofocus. 35mm compact camera, f2.8 38mm lens, automatic focusing, automatic programmed exposure, shutter 1/60-1/360.

The happy parent or teacher, invited or forced to accompany a class on an outdoor nature study will do well to remember the camera. This is the ideal opportunity to observe and record the temporarily relaxed behaviour of schoolchildren, and their natural segregation between the sexes. A camera will generally be accepted as long as it does not interfere with proceedings, hence familiarity with equipment and rapid operation are essentials to success. As in most child photography, fast films and shutter speeds may be useful.

Boys and girls do not attach the same importance to the subject of nature study. Girls (with some exceptions – above left), will form groups eager to absorb knowledge on the indigenous flora. Boys on the other hand may have a somewhat more worldly outlook, engaging in various extra-mural activities. The troubled frowns and toothless grins of these future pillars of our society are well worth capturing.

IN PRAISE OF THE SNAPSHOT

are returned from the developing and processing laboratory, and dotting the envelopes all over the house – at the back of the drawer in the kitchen table, the top right-hand drawer of the chest of drawers, and the shelf at the top of the wardrobe, to name but three favourite hiding places.

The easiest method is to put the envelopes in a large cardboard box (which you can then put at the bottom of the wardrobe). They are not too accessible, but it is fun to fossick through them from time to time, and if you desperately need a picture you can usually find it in an hour or so, and have a lot of fun looking. This may sound rather tongue in cheek, but a friend of mine who is a brilliant artist and singer stores all her pictures like this (except for a few in a scrapbook and a few in frames) and swears by it. To save excessive confusion at a later date, try dating the outsides of the envelopes.

A slightly tidier approach uses an expanding file, or even one of those miniature filing cabinets sold for organising household papers (or <u>bills</u>, as we say); I use this together with albums, scrapbooks, and various ways of hanging pictures on the wall.

Scrapbooks are cheap and fun, but eventually the acid-containing paper from which most of them are made will cause prints to fade. Proper albums, provided they come from a reputable maker, are very much safer and also very much more

New York, or for that matter any city in the grip of winter, provides a wealth of snapshot opportunities, whether you happen to live there or are just visiting. Left: A blizzard empties the normally teeming streets of traffic, the occasional commuter showing his determination not to be beaten. Heavy, snow-laden skies reduce the buildings to a monochromatic impression of their former selves. Below left: The low sun casts long shadows on the ice, where skaters take uncertain, knife-edge steps. Below: The dramatic blue of the sky provides a suitable backdrop to the soaring skyline that surrounds Central Park. Facing page: Not to be missed are the shots of children playing in the snow, the clear air and all-pervading white heightening the vivid colours of their clothes.

Photographing snow scenes can pose unforeseen problems. Light conditions may vary dramatically, so it is worth being prepared for all eventualities by loading the camera with a fast film. 400ASA should give adequate flexibility by allowing movement to be frozen and enabling shots to be taken in dull conditions. When determining exposure, remember that both manual and automatic systems may be fooled by the large expanse of white, leading to under-exposure. Try to meter on your subject, or use the camera's compensation device. A fast film will be more tolerant of any errors. A skylight filter fitted to your lens will prevent the pictures from appearing too blue, and will protect the optics.

Kodak 160 EF. PR10 instant print film,
fixed focus lens, automatic programmed exposure,
print lighten/darken facility, shutter 2-1/300,
built-in electronic flash.

expensive, so only get used for rather more important pictures as far as I am concerned. My brother, on the other hand, makes up very carefully sequenced albums containing only the very best of his pictures (and he takes far fewer than I do), throwing the second-best into a cardboard box. Over the years, such a set of albums can become a treasure.

For display, there are three approaches, formal, semi-formal, and informal. The formal approach uses frames, either hanging on the wall or free-standing. These are particularly suitable for pictures of children or wives or whatever – essentially, for portraits. They are also ideal as presents for grandparents and the like. Consider enlargements, too, if the negative will stand it.

Bigger pictures are almost always more attractive than smaller ones.

The semi-formal approach uses cardboard folders, which can either stand up like Christmas cards, providing a cheap equivalent to frames, or protect the picture whilst it is stored in a drawer. Finally, the informal approach uses Blu-Tack or simply pins on a notice-type board: this is the approach which I favour, as a constantly-changing display is very easy and always refreshing. Incidentally, it is worth using the same board for other pictures, clipped from magazines or any other source. As a means of increasing your visual awareness, which is what successful photography is all about, this is unbeatable.

IN PRAISE OF THE SNAPSHOT

However you display colour prints, they will eventually fade. Some take very much longer than others, depending on the conditions of display and the type of materials used. If you value a print, and want to keep it on display, make sure that you know where the negative is. Alternatively, consider slides.

Although the vast majority of snapshots are taken on colour negative (print) film, the colour slide is alive and well. Suggestions to help you choose which to use are given in the next chapter, but if you do decide to use slides, remember the following guidelines when planning a slide show.

First, edit ruthlessly. Winnow out all duplicates and near-duplicates. This not only makes the show more interesting, it also makes it shorter – and whilst most people will find a ten or twenty minute show interesting, anything longer is likely to lose you more friends than it makes.

Secondly, get the slides in some kind of sequence. Begin (after the fashion of Alice in Wonderland) at the beginning, go on until you reach the end, and then stop. A show which begins with a few shots beside the pool, then goes back to the airport when you were setting out – or was it coming back? No, these are the ones where we were coming back . . . – and then a picture of the place we were staying . . . This kind of shambles is tiring and uninformative to watch.

Thirdly, rehearse beforehand. Make sure that all the slides are the right way up. Professionals do this by 'spotting,' or sticking coloured (and sometimes numbered) spots in the <u>bottom left-hand</u> corner of the slide when it is held in the hand and 'reading' correctly (right way up and right way round). On projection, these spots will (if you are sitting behind the projector) be in the top right-hand corner facing towards you. Make sure that you can say <u>something</u> intelligent about each slide – if you can't, either remove it or keep quiet whilst it is on the screen. Notes, or even a written script, may help. Run the slides through and see how long they need on the screen: some can stand considerably longer exposure than others. In any case, a maximum time of ten or fifteen seconds is enough, and many slides need only be on the screen for five seconds.

This may seem like a lot of trouble, but it is worth doing even for family-only shows: and once you are used to it, you will become painfully aware of the shortcomings of those who are less well-organised.

Driving across an unfamiliar land, it is worth keeping one's eyes open for the unusual sights, and stopping when a snapshot opportunity presents itself. **Above:** Elephant handlers and their hard-working charges pause for a well-earned rest in a Burmese village, ignoring the attention of the tourists' camera. **Right:** Two of New York's finest exchange a few words before continuing with their duties. Policemen are accustomed to being photographed, and will not generally object unless you interfere with their work in your search for the more unusual shot. Both pictures show everyday sights in their own setting, and yet will be uncommon to the outsider, who may see this as the reason for their appeal.

Yashica MG1. 35mm camera with f2.8 45mm lens, rangefinder focusing, aperture priority automatic exposure, shutter 2-1/500, delayed action.

The beauty of the modern camera is that it is generally small, many slipping easily into pocket or handbag, and simple to use. This being so, there is no reason why they should not be carried at all times rather than just on special occasions. Ready at a moment's notice, they will record any sights that we may find appealing. The pictures **left and bottom** show the type of character shots that can be captured at home or abroad. **Below:** A typical holiday snap that will serve as a talking point when shown to friends on one's return home.

FILM

It may seem strange to consider the film before the camera: but after all, the camera is only a machine for exposing the film, and if we understand the film's requirements we can see what the camera must do in order to meet them.

The original black-and-white films were based on a simple discovery made in the eighteenth century: certain silver-containing chemicals (silver salts) go black when exposed to light. In the nineteenth century, ways were found of using this effect to get photographs: the most difficult part was <u>fixing</u> the image, so that further exposure to light had no effect.

In the present century, colour photography using coloured dyes became possible. The theory behind it is frighteningly complex, but basically what happens is that the film consists of three layers sensitised to the three primary colours. Each is a conventional silver-based film, but contains in addition colour couplers, so that as the black-and-white image is formed, so is a dye image. When the silver image is chemically removed, only the dyes are left behind. Because any colour can be duplicated by mixing the three primaries, the final picture is a fair imitation of the original scene. This applies to colour slide film: for colour negative film, different dyes are used, but the principle is the same.

An important thing to remember is that a colour picture can <u>only</u> be a fair imitation of the original scene. For a start, it is two-dimensional instead of three-dimensional. Also, the colours are not the <u>actual</u> colours; they are just a combination of dyes which give the same impression. If you remember this, you can manipulate the limitations of the process to give the impression that you want. If you forget it – well, the classic example is the grandeur of a mountain scene, which looks a lot less impressive when reduced to a 3″ x 4½″ piece of coloured paper!

Although black-and-white film still has an immense and loyal following, it is rather a specialised market. In the first place, anyone who wants good quality from black-and-white has to do his own processing, or use an expensive custom black-and-white lab. The competition in colour processing means that black-and-white is no longer cheaper than colour: if anything, the reverse is true!

Nevertheless, black-and-white photography has a quality all of its own, and if you like the effects you may wish to consider using it. It is also vastly more permanent than any colour process. An archivally processed black-and-white print has a life measured in centuries or even millenia. Taking pictures for posterity may seem pretentious – but what would you give for an

Polaroid SX70 Alpha I Model 2. SX70 instant print film.
Folding single lens reflex, automatic programmed exposure,
print lighten or darken facility, shutter 14-1/180.

The common link between all the pictures shown on these pages is their considerable depth of field. This is normally desired in general views, where near and distant objects are to appear equally sharp. This can be achieved by selecting the smallest aperture possible, assuming your camera allows this. This done, focus should be set to maximise the effect, and a careful study of the scale of your lens will indicate the distances between which objects will seem sharp at a given aperture. In obtaining this effect, keep an eye on shutter speed to avoid blur.

Facing page: The striped yellow/red sails of the beached boats were seen as a good way of adding colour to a predominantly blue-green background. In the scenes **top left and above,** flowers served the same purpose. These shots demonstrate the importance of choosing your viewpoint in order to make your pictures more interesting. **Left:** By shooting from beneath the overhanging branches of a palm tree, the photographer was able to provide an attractive frame to his picture, which also helped relieve the regular lines of sand, sea and sky.

FILM

everyday album of pictures showing your grandfather's life?

The first of the modern colour films was Kodachrome, introduced in 1936 (1935 for movies). Like the modern Kodachrome, it was a slide film. Slide films have many advantages: their colours can be very faithful, they can give the impression of quite a long brightness range from bright sunlight to shadow, they can be projected and shown to very large audiences and processing is quicker, easier, and cheaper than for colour prints.

On the other hand, slides have two major drawbacks. The first is that you need a projector to appreciate them fully – prints are certainly more convenient for showing to friends – and the second is that exposure is much more critical than with negative films.

There are also various minor disadvantages, such as the fact that you are dealing with an original: if a slide is damaged (and even a dirty fingerprint can write a slide off, which is why so many professionals mount slides between glass) it is ruined, whereas a ruined print can be remade from the negative. 'Dupes,' or duplicate slides, seldom equal the originals in quality, and any colour casts or minor inaccuracies in exposure cannot be corrected during printing as they can with negative film.

The question of colour casts is particularly important if you are taking pictures under different light sources. Although the human eye can adjust to almost any reasonably white light source, it is common experience that the light from an ordinary domestic light-bulb is much yellower than daylight. A colour film cannot adjust in the same way as the human eye, and so it has to be 'balanced' for a particular light source – usually daylight or photoflood. Photofloods are special photographic lamps, which run rather hotter than an ordinary domestic bulb. They give off rather more light than domestic lamps, and their colour is slightly more blue: they also have a shorter life.

Above: A Bateau Mouche pleasure craft provides a good way of photographing the majesty of Paris. *Top: Venice's* famous Rialto bridge spans the Grand Canal, where gondolas and vaporettos provide the usual means of transport. No shots of this unique city would be complete without a picture of these. *Right: Manhattan's* towers reflected in the still waters of a lake in Central Park.

Nikon EM. 35mm single lens reflex, taking most Nikon A.I. fit lenses. Aperture priority automatic exposure, shutter 1-1/1000, delayed action. Accepts dedicated flash and film winder.

You may have noticed that there has been no reference to fluorescent lighting. This is because fluorescent tubes are not strictly comparable to daylight or tungsten light sources (light bulbs). Correction filters which will allow an acceptable result are available for use with both daylight (FL-D) and artificial light (FL-A) films, but you must not expect anything better than merely acceptable results.

Of course, all of the above only applies to single types of light source. If you try to take a picture under mixed light sources, it is impossible to guarantee acceptable results. To take a really bad example, imagine an office with large windows and supplementary fluorescent lighting and a desk lamp on the

Left: Photogenic in itself, the Eiffel tower is the ideal spot from which to capture the whole panorama of the city. Below: On fine days, an ever present rainbow spans the boiling waters of Niagara Falls. There are plenty of points from which to photograph the falls, but if doing so from the "Maid of the Mist," remember to protect your camera from the spray.

FILM

Canon AF 35M. 35mm compact camera, f2.8 38mm lens, automatic focusing, automatic programmed exposure, shutter 1/8-1/500, motorised film advance and re-wind, delayed action, built-in flash.

The family cat, considering its lofty position in the household, demands our photographic attention. Like children, cats are subject to changes of mood, and these are well worth capturing on film. The primary rules to pet photography are: familiarity with your animal and timing. Without these, all you are likely to get is a tail at the edge of the frame. A fast shutter speed will avoid pictures being spoilt by sudden movement, so, good lighting, and even flash, will help. You may find yourself following Felix around on your knees, but patience reaps rewards.

Hanimex 35MF. 35mm compact camera, f4 38mm lens, symbol focusing, automatic exposure, shutter 1/125, built-in motor wind and electronic flash.

subject's desk. A professional trapped in this circumstance would simply give up, and use powerful electronic flashguns to supplement the daylight and drown out the fluorescents, possibly replacing the lamp in the desk light with a 275W photoflood to give a pool of yellow light where it was needed.

Given, then, that colour negative films are convenient, easy, cheap, and overcome at least some of the problems with different types of lighting (though they are not too good on fluorescents and cannot handle mixed light sources), what are the disadvantages?

The worst is that colour prints do not last. A colour print on open display in bright light may have a life of only a few months before it begins to fade, and the colours go awry. Even in a nice cool dark album, there will be a detectable change within a few years – maybe as few as five or ten, maybe as many as thirty or forty. The only way to arrest this is to freeze the image, and indeed it is becoming quite usual for professionals to store colour negatives and slides in a freezer!

A lesser drawback is that unless you pay quite a lot of money, you may get colour casts on your prints. These come

*Top: **Goat and child deep in** conversation. **Left:** Sights such as this crocodile of Parisian children are a snapshot must. **Below and bottom:** The mutual affection between girl and dog was an irresistible subject. When shooting against the light, as below, avoid a dark result by adjusting exposure. **Facing page top:** The dappled sunlight through the trees adds further interest to such a shot. **Bottom:** Children at play are oblivious to the camera.*

about because the automatic printers used in colour processing labs are set to 'integrate to grey'. This means that they are set to deal with an <u>average</u> picture, which comes out to an <u>average</u> overall colour. They can deal perfectly with <u>average</u> subjects (such as a portrait taken in the open with some blue sky and green grass), but if you depart much from this, the machine tries to force the overall average colour back to its pre-set norm, and gives you a colour cast.

There are other minor drawbacks, too – the unsuitability of prints for a large audience, and the inability of colour negative films to resolve such fine detail as black-and-white or colour slide films – but these are not in the least bit important for snapshots, so on balance the colour print film wins hands down.

It may seem strange to have devoted a good part of this chapter to telling you something you had decided anyway, but there is method in this approach. First of all, the pressure against colour prints from photo-snobs is immense: most 'serious amateurs' would rather die than use 'snapshot' film. Secondly, it is distressingly common for snapshotters to be fobbed off with

FILM

excuses from processing labs. Sometimes the reasons why pictures do not live up to your expectations are inherent in the process – mixed lighting, for example. On other occasions, colour casts are sheer carelessness on the part of the lab, often resulting from not checking the colour characteristics of a new batch of paper when reloading the machines, and you can quite reasonably demand to have them reprinted. Finally, if you understand a bit about how films work, you are less likely to make as many mistakes in using them in the first place.

Apart from the choice of film type, there are a few other film characteristics to consider: film speed and graininess, film care, and film processing.

Film speed is a measure of how much light a film needs in order to record an image. A <u>slow</u> film requires a lot of light, and a <u>fast</u> film requires less. Film speeds are measured in a number of ways, but the most usual is ANSI (American National Standards Institute), more usually known under its old name of ASA (American Standards Association). In a straightforward American manner, ANSI/ASA speeds are arithmetic in progression: 400 ASA is four times as sensitive as 100 ASA. The other widely used system is the German DIN (Deutsche Industrie Normen), which is logarithmic: a doubling

of speed means an increase of 3 in the speed index. A 100 ASA film is equivalent to 21 DIN, so 200 ASA is 24 DIN and 400 ASA is 27 DIN.

Slide films begin at ASA 25 (15 DIN); the most popular speed is ASA 64 (19 DIN), with some at 100 ASA (21 DIN). Fast slide films are available at 200 ASA (24 DIN) and 400 ASA (27 DIN) with an artificial-light-only film from 3M at 650 ASA (29 DIN).

At any given speed, the choice of brand is a matter of personal preference. Each maker has his own particular type of colour – contrasty or soft, with perhaps a slight reddish bias (characteristic of some Japanese films) or brownish (German) or bluish (American). Bearing in mind what was said about a picture being no more than a fair representation, you must simply pick the one which you like most (or dislike least).

Colour print films, with few exceptions, are either 100 ASA (21 DIN) or 400 ASA (27 DIN). Although 100 ASA is fine for most purposes, the extra speed of the 400 ASA means that you can photograph in poor light without using flash. The fast films also have more <u>latitude</u> against over- or under- exposure, and a considerably better tolerance of mixed lighting sources (this is also true of fast colour slide films). Although it is rather more

Yashica MF-2. 35mm compact camera with f4 38mm lens, fixed focus, fixed exposure, shutter 1/125, built-in electronic flash.

expensive to buy a 400 ASA film than a 100 ASA one (processing and printing cost the same), many people use them as standard snapshot films.

With colour negative films, the brand chosen is not particularly important: colour variations between makes are less noticeable than colour variations between different processing labs. At a given speed, all tend to be similar in graininess.

For the usual small snapshot enlargements, the grain is invisible from both 100 ASA and 400 ASA, but the bigger the enlargement, the more apparent the difference becomes. A 100 ASA film enlarged from 35mm to 8 x 10″ gives virtually invisible grain, but it shows up at 20 x 16″; with 400 ASA film, the grain structure is visible at 10 x 8.″

This, of course, assumes that you use 35mm film. If you use the much larger rollfilms, the magnifications are less and grain is invisible even at 20 x 16,″ but if you use 110 it is readily visible even at 10 x 8″: in fact, the quality of a postcard-sized print from 110 is about the same as 10 x 8″ print from 35mm. At 10 x 8″ and larger, the image can be so broken up by the grain of the film when using 400 ASA 110 film that fine detail vanishes to quite a distressing extent. If you use 126 film, the results are similar to 35mm.

Facing page: A little forward planning will ensure that you do not miss the stage-coach. Select your viewpoint beforehand and focus on the spot where your subject will appear. If operating a manual camera, pre-arrange your exposure making sure that the shutter speed is adequate to stop the motion. With subject approaching, follow it through your viewfinder into the planned position. This panning will help stop the movement and will ensure that there is no cut-off in the resulting picture. ***Top left:*** A lucky shot; the powder-flash from a musket barrel recorded with the help of perfect anticipation. ***Above:*** Killer whales rise to the bait to produce a unique snap. ***Left:*** Historic shows provide a wealth of colour.

FILM

The very small format has other disadvantages, too. First, any dirt or fingerprints acquired during processing are blown up much more than on 35mm or larger formats – this can be even worse when ordering reprints. Secondly, because the degree of enlargement is so great, any defects in the quality of the lens are shown up mercilessly. The lens on a 10 x 8″ camera need not have a very high resolving power at all, especially if a contact print is made: but in order to get a 10 x 8″ print from a 110 negative, a 15x enlargement is required, so the resolving power of the lens must be fifteen times as great as for the larger camera. Thirdly, exposures must be more accurate: overexposure (the standard practice with negative film) results in larger grain and worse resolution, which may not matter too much on 35mm but can tip the balance on 110.

On 35mm and rollfilm cameras, and a few cartridge-loading types, the film speed has to be set by the photographer, but many cartridge-loading cameras (110 and 126) automatically set the film speed by means of a key on the cartridge.

Of course, the reference to setting the film speed assumes that your camera has some sort of meter. If it does not, then there are two possibilities. One is that it is a simple box camera, and relies on the latitude of the film (its ability to accept under and overexposure) to cover up exposure errors: such cameras can only be used out of doors, in good light, or with a flash. They are set so that on a cloudy day, the exposure is more-or-less correct: on a sunny day, the film is simply overexposed!

The carefree atmosphere of a winter sports resort is a stimulus to the happy snap. Whether you decide to show the halting steps of the beginner experiencing skis for the first time, or the graceful skills of the accomplished performer, you are unlikely to find a shortage of subjects. The attention grabbing colours of the clothes will appear more vivid in the dazzling light of a cloudless sky. Pictures taken at altitude under these bright conditions may appear blue. To avoid this, fit an ultra-violet absorbing filter to your lens. Unlike other filters, it will not affect exposure. A lens hood is useful in keeping unwanted light away from the lens, and will help you get a brighter picture. Compact cameras that fit the pocket of an anorak are ideal, whereas larger equipment hung from the neck can be dangerous in a fall.

Kodak Disc 4000, disc cartridge film loading, f2.8 12.5mm lens, fixed focus, automatic exposure, shutter 1/100-1/200, motorised film advance, built-in electronic flash.

FILM

The second possibility is that you can set the various controls, as described in the next chapter, but that you need a separate meter or at least an exposure guide (such as the one packed with the film) to do so. A fairly comprehensive exposure guide is given in the next chapter.

No matter what make, size, or speed of film you use (and it is worth familiarising yourself with one and sticking to it), it has to be looked after. The expiry date on the box is there for a reason: as film gets older, the colour balance changes, and it often loses some of its sensitivity. Provided the film is well stored, there is quite a bit of latitude in this date and the film will be quite usable for a few months after the expiry date. If it is badly stored, though, it can deteriorate seriously even before the expiry date. The worst thing is heat, and at 100-120°F (quite easily reached on the rear window of a car) even a few <u>hours</u> can have a noticeable effect: certainly, repeated treatment of this kind will have very marked effects. Before using the film, keep it somewhere cool and whilst it is in the camera, keep that cool too. Excessive humidity, too, can damage film and make it more prone to scratching, so keep exposed and unexposed film in a dry place.

Ideally, you should have the film processed as soon as possible after exposing it, as the latent image slowly fades. To take the worst possible case, pictures taken in the spring and left in the camera during a hot summer, with the kind of ill-treatment described above, will almost certainly be mottled and unpleasantly coloured when they are developed and printed.

Where do you get the film processed? The best results, and easily the most expensive, come from labs which cater primarily for the professional photographer, but these can cost two or three times as much as the cheapest and produce results no better than a good cheap lab. What you do get, though, is reliability and repeatability. The very cheapest are usually a bit less careful both in processing and in checking the prints afterwards, but some of the best work I have ever had on colour film came from a lab which was only a few pennies more expensive for 36 prints than the cheapest advertised. They were repeated winners of the Kodak Quality Awards, and if you can find a lab which can boast this you are well on the way to a winner.

Incidentally, the old rules about not printing pictures which showed nudes are now very much relaxed: unless your pictures are so revealing as to be bordering on the pornographic, there will be no problem from any lab.

I prefer to use a local processor rather than mail order, for two reasons. The first is that the chances of losing the film are greatly reduced, and the second is that if there is something wrong with the pictures, it is much easier to remonstrate face to face (and to refuse to pay until they get it right) than it is by letter.

If they do get it wrong – and this usually takes the form of an unacceptable colour cast – you can gauge a lot from the way they react. If someone tells me that no-one else has complained, and that the pictures are perfectly all right, when this is patently a lie, I get rather angry and never go there again. Refuse to pay if you think that they are giving you the run-around, and ask that they submit the film to Kodak, (or other manufacturer) if you are convinced that you are right. Remember though, that you may have made a mistake: the most usual one is under-exposure, which is detectable as thin, washed-out negatives. If you are wrong, have the grace to admit it!

A guide book purchased at the zoo will contain splendid pictures of the animals, and yet these are no substitute for your own efforts which, even if inferior, will give considerable pleasure. Excellent results can be had even without special facilities, so it is well-worth trying your hand and taking a little time and care in your photography. A reflex camera with long lens is useful in reaching the more timid, distant or dangerous animals, but even the more modest fixed lens equipment can provide the perfect animal snap. Get as near as possible to the cages and enclosures. If possible,

position the lens between the bars and allow for subject movement when setting your shutter speed. Close-meshed grilles need not be a deterrent. Select a wide aperture and place the lens against the mesh – it will not show in the picture. If long lenses are being used, particularly at wide apertures, remember that depth of field will be very limited, so take extra care in focusing.

Olympus Pen EF. 35mm compact camera,
half frame format, f3.5 28mm lens,
fixed focus, automatic exposure, shutter 1/60-1/250,
built-in electronic flash.

CAMERAS

The film captures the picture; it is the camera's job to get the picture onto the film.

The first essential of a camera is the lens. True, a pinhole will give you an image – but it will not be a very sharp one, and it allows so little light through that a very long exposure indeed would be needed to record the image on the film.

The lens then, has two functions. One is to focus the image sharply, and the other is to let the light through in sufficient quantity. Whilst a simple lens consisting of a single piece of glass can provide an image, and certainly lets plenty of light through, the image quality is not very good. The resolution of fine detail is poor, straight lines come out curved, and the image at the edge of the field of view may be barely recognisable.

To get around these objections, it is usual to combine several separate simple lenses (also called elements) to make a single compound, complex lens.

At this point, it is necessary to explain how lens speed is measured. We have all seen the usual figures – f:2, f:2.8, f:4, f:5.6 and so on, and a pretty strange set they are. They are worked out by dividing the focal length of the lens into its absolute aperture.

The focal length is easily understood. As children, most of us focused the sun with a magnifying-glass to set fire to leaves

Above: **With tourism so** *important to the economy of the Hawaiian islands, it is no surprise that so much of the entertainment is geared exclusively towards the visitor. Shown here is the Kodak Hawaii Hula show, which attracts many spectators to Waikiki Shell on the island of Oahu.* **Left:** *A popcorn stall may not sound much like snapshot material, but then this one is a little more ornate than most. Seemingly oblivious of the photographer's attention, the stall-holders concentrate on business. It is worth noting that the picture concentrates on just a small part of the vehicle, and by doing so focuses attention, in an effective way, on the finer details of the carriage. The same technique can be used creatively on many other subjects.* **Facing page & Top left:** *A Mexican woman tends a fresh-fruit stall, with the beautifully prepared pineapple on ice looking as good as it must taste. Having made one's purchase, take a shot of the display. It will remind you of what fruit should taste like.* **Top right:** *American-style Yeoman obligingly poses for the family camera.* **Bottom:** *Another Hawaiian tourist orientated display on the waters of Coco Palms lagoon.*

Cosina CX-2. 35mm compact camera, f2.8 35mm lens, symbol/scale focusing, automatic programmed exposure, shutter 2-1/500, delayed action. Film winder and dedicated flash available.

CAMERAS

and pieces of paper. To get it to work, we had to hold the lens at a precise distance from the paper. The sun is effectively infinitely far away – 93,000,000 miles – and a typical magnifying glass has to be held at about 6″ from the paper to focus the sun's rays; thus we say that the <u>focal length</u> of the magnifying glass is 6.″ In one way, a photographic objective lens is no more than a glorified magnifying glass, and has to be held a set distance from the film in order to focus an image of distant objects onto it. On a 35mm camera, the focal length of the lens is usually about 2.″ In other words, distant objects are sharply focused on the film when the lens is held 2″ away from it.

The absolute aperture is, despite its forbidding name, even simpler. It is no more than the diameter of the lens. If the lens aperture (not the mount) is 1″ across, then the absolute aperture is 1.″

If we divide the <u>focal length</u> (2″ in our example) into the <u>absolute aperture</u> (1″ in our example) we get ½. This is also expressed as f1:2 or f/2.

A little thought will show that the <u>smaller</u> the absolute aperture, the <u>larger</u> the f:no will be. Sticking with the 2″ lens, a ½″ aperture gives us f/4 and a ¼″ aperture is f/8. Going the other way, a 2″ aperture would be f/1. These f:nos are referred to as <u>relative apertures</u> or more simply as <u>stops</u>.

So far, we have only considered the maximum aperture of the lens. Almost all lenses for practical use incorporate an <u>iris diaphragm,</u> by which means the size of the aperture may be controlled. Typically, an f/2 lens on a 35mm camera might <u>stop down</u> to f/16 in the following increments: f/2 . . . f/2.8 . . . f/4 . . . f/5.6 . . . f/8 . . . f/11 . . . f/16.

This not only controls the amount of light reaching the film (and remember that we want to guard against overexposure as well as against underexposure), it also affects the <u>depth of field,</u> which is the range over which subjects appear sharp.

So-called 'fixed focus' cameras take advantage of this by using a very small stop (f/9 or smaller) and allowing the resultant depth-of-field to take the place of focusing.

The lens stop is one way of affecting how much light reaches the film, and the other is the shutter. On a good camera, speeds from 1 full second (or even longer) down to 1/1000 second (or even shorter) will be available, together with a 'B' ('Brief' or 'Bulb') setting which holds the shutter open for as long as the shutter release is kept depressed.

As with the diaphragm, changing the shutter speed does more than just changing the amount of light coming through. It also affects the action-stopping ability of the camera. At 1/1000, all but the fastest motion is 'frozen', whereas at 1/30 quite serious blur may be seen in fast-moving subjects. At speeds longer than 1/30, most people have difficulty in holding the camera still and the movement of the photographer (<u>camera shake</u>) becomes as important as subject movement, so a tripod or other support becomes necessary.

Top: A snapshotter and his model attracted the attention of the photographer, who had noticed the interest being shown in the proceedings by the child on the sun lounger. Centre: A combination of high viewpoint and wide angle lens provided the desired result in this picture of relaxation in the garden of *an English pub. Right: Asked to pose in front of the camera a subject may appear rigid and awkward. A prop will literally provide support that will lead to a more natural-looking shot. Facing page: A delightful shot of girl and dog searching the waters of a cove for crabs.*

Ricoh 500 RF. 35mm compact camera, f2.8 40mm lens,
rangefinder focusing, shutter priority automatic exposure,
manual override, shutter 1/8-1/500,
delayed action. Accepts accessory film winder.

CAMERAS

Below: Alkmaar cheese market in Holland provides sights that are unusual to all but the Dutch, with its sledge-like barrows and their white-clad porters. Right: The Sacré-Coeur on Montmarte from Place du Tertre. Relaxing over a coffee, it is worth surveying the neighbourhood for shots in an area that attracts artists from all over the world. *Bottom: No visit to Holland in the spring would be complete without a photograph of the endless rows of tulips to be seen in parks and countryside. Shown here is the Keukenhof flower exhibition.*

Fujica Auto 5. 35mm compact camera, f2.8 38mm lens, scale focusing, automatic programmed exposure, shutter 1/8-1/500, delayed action, built-in motor wind and electronic flash.

Top left: Taken from the balcony of a hotel in Acapulco, this shot shows the interesting whale-like shape of the pool below, surrounded by rows of sun beds that echo its curve. A similar shot from the window of a holiday hotel will serve as a good reminder of the happy vacation. **Above:** Sea World attracts visitors from all over the world, its performing animals a delight and wonder to both children and adults. Here killer whales demonstrate an uncanny response to human command. For best results when photographing such subjects, take the picture when the animal is at the peak of its jump. **Left:** A wide angle lens was used to record the pre-match activity at a baseball game in Philadelphia. Such lenses have the effect of making enclosed areas look somewhat larger than they really are. Most compact cameras are fitted with medium wide angle lenses that, together with their depth of field characteristics, make them ideal for this type of snap.

CAMERAS

The shutter is arranged in steps which halve (or double) the amount of light passing: thus 1/60 second allows twice as much light to pass as 1/125, but only half as much as 1/30. By using the shutter speed dial and the aperture ring together, the photographer can decide how much action-stopping he wants, and how much depth-of-field: stopping down for increased depth of field entails longer shutter speeds, with more risk of subject movement or camera shake, and using higher shutter speeds inevitably involves wider apertures and less depth of field. Thus, all these exposures are equivalent:
1/1000 at f/2…1/500 at f/2.8…1/250 at f/4…1/125 at f/5.6 . . . 1/60 at f/8 . . . 1/30 at f/11 . . . 1/15 at f/16.

Which you choose depends on the effect you want. A good all-purpose compromise might be 1/125 at f/5.6 but if you were photographing fast moving cars 1/1000 at f/2 might be more appropriate, or if you particularly wanted to keep everything in focus from as near as possible to as far as possible, a tripod and 1/15 at f/16 would be more useful.

Although traditionally the photographer sets both speed and aperture independently, it is becoming more and more usual to have some form of automation. Typically, the photographer sets the aperture, and the camera sets the speed: in the example above, if you set f/5.6 the camera would set 1/125 for you. Furthermore, it would change that speed if the sun went in behind a cloud, or if the weather suddenly brightened. In the vast majority of snapshot conditions, such automation will result in correctly exposed pictures, but there can be two problems. First, you may set too small an aperture, so the camera gives too long an exposure to stop subject movement or camera shake – this is known in the trade as 'the perfectly exposed blur.' Secondly, in awkward conditions – a dark subject with bright surroundings, or vice versa – the meter will be fooled, and is likely to give you the wrong exposure; but we shall look at this later.

Another form of automation is the so called <u>shutter-priority</u> (the type already described is called <u>aperture-priority</u>). Here, you set the shutter and the camera sets the aperture.

A third type of automation alters both shutter speed and aperture according to a pre-set programme built into the camera by its manufacturers. Whilst this is fine for the vast majority of snapshot pictures, it can be very limiting if you have some particular effect in mind which involves action-stopping shutter speeds or accurately-controlled depth of field.

Wherever you happen to go as tourist, day-tripper or holidaymaker, the chances are that others will also have been drawn there. **Far right and top:** Tour groups and their guides pictured against a backdrop of ancient architectural splendour. Note the high viewpoint chosen behind the groups so as to show both people and setting. **Right:** A similar shot, but set against a modern skyline.

The only other main camera feature we have not considered so far is the viewfinder – after all, it is essential to have at least some idea of what you are photographing. The earliest Kodaks merely provided a couple of sighting grooves, but nowadays things are a bit more sophisticated. The wire or stamped-metal frame finder which used to be so popular on box cameras and folders is now rarely met with, and the same applies

Konica C35 AF2. 35mm compact camera,
f2.8 38mm lens, automatic focusing, automatic programmed exposure,
shutter 1/60-1/250, built-in electronic flash.

Left: The Horseguards in London's Whitehall are an imposing sight ever popular with visitors to the city. Children in particular like to admire the animals and gaze in wonder at the silent, unmoving rider in his shining finery. In this typical photograph of a class of school children, the location is established by simply including the horse's head and passing buses in the picture. **Below:** Feeding the pigeons is a popular activity in most major cities. These tame urban birds fascinate adults and children alike by their approachability, and not surprisingly such scenes are a common subject for the snapshot. In this picture of visitors to Amsterdam's Dam Square, a wide angle lens was used to show as much of the setting as possible whilst keeping the subject group in close-up. A low viewpoint is preferable for children and crouching figures.

CAMERAS

to the 'brilliant' reflecting finder: which is just as well, because both of these contrivances gave no more than a rough idea of where the camera was pointing.

Nowadays, there are four types of finder. The first is a simple optical finder. These are fine beyond about six feet, but closer than that you begin to run into parallax problems: the viewfinder and the taking lens are inevitably a little distance apart, and consequently the image in the viewfinder does not correspond exactly to the image on the film: this can lead to the famous 'chopped-off-heads' effect if you do not make allowances at close distances, making sure that nothing of importance is too close to the top of the viewfinder.

Rather more sophisticated is the brightline finder, in which the field of view appears as a suspended white or golden line. Whilst this can give rise to similar parallax problems to the plain optical finder, it may have one of two aids to avoid this. The simpler one is a subsidiary brightline, to be used when taking close-ups: this is just below the main brightline, and is usually dotted or partial to distinguish it from the main one. A more complex (and expensive) system actually moves the brightline as you are focusing, so that the field of view of the finder and of the lens coincide at all times.

A third type of finder, widely used in high-quality cameras, is that employed in the single-lens reflex. This has the enormous advantage that you see exactly what the lens sees, and that you can change lenses without the need for extra viewfinders. It also means that focusing and viewing are automatically combined, whereas with direct-vision finders like those described above it is possible to compose the picture without focusing – though we shall say more about focusing aids later.

Whereas in the single-lens-reflex (SLR) the mirror swings out of the way for the exposure, in the twin-lens-reflex there are once again two lenses, one for the camera and one for the viewfinder. Although viewing and focusing can be combined in the same way as for the SLR, the parallax problems remain, though a moving mask takes care of them down to about three feet (the closest focusing distance of most non-SLR cameras).

Apart from reflex focusing (whether SLR or TLR) there are three other ways of setting focus. The first is scale focusing, where you guess the distance and set it on a scale on the lens; some engrave actual distances, and others use symbols such as a head for close-ups, a full-length figure for middle distances, and a range of mountains for infinity.

The second employs a coupled rangefinder. These cameras are distinguishable by their extra viewfinder window on the front. When you look through the viewfinder, the middle of the field of view is split in two. As you focus the lens, the split image moves closer together, and when the two images coincide exactly, the

Chinon CA-4. 35mm single lens reflex, f1.9 50mm lens. Accepts K-mount lenses, aperture priority automatic exposure, shutter 1-1/1000, delayed action.

camera is focused upon the subject covered by the rangefinder.

The third is <u>automatic focusing</u>. This can be achieved in a number of ways from the technical point of view, but they are all similar in use. A small area of the viewfinder is marked out, much like the rangefinder patch in a manually focused camera, and the camera automatically focuses on this. Whilst this system is perfect for many snapshots, it has a couple of drawbacks. The first is that unless you have some sort of prefocusing lock or manual override you can only focus on the subject in the middle of the picture – which may not be the best approach aesthetically. The second is that all auto-focus systems can be fooled, though it depends on the system used what fools them. Some cannot focus through glass, and others are confused in various ways by foreground material such as overhanging foliage or railings.

As with exposure automation, focus automation is a boon for the simplest of snapshots but does involve the surrender of a certain amount of control by the photographer; if you can live with this, there is little doubt that autofocus cameras make snapshots easier than they have ever been before.

CAMERA TYPES

Having looked at the essentials of the camera, we can now look at the different camera types. There are four basic types likely to be used for snapshots, though as already mentioned almost any

*Facing page: Don't forget the camera when carnival time comes. Milling crowds, happy faces and unbelievable costumes will be there in profusion, all good snapshot opportunities. Night-time shots such as shown, will require flash. A small camera is a must if you are joining in the fun, and a compact, with built-in flash is fine, but remember the limited power and get in close. **Top left:** A happy girl pictured at home aboard a Hong Kong junk. **Left:** Long lens and high viewpoint were used to obtain this rather unusual photograph of a gondolier relaxing aboard his craft. Take the shot even if you can't get close, you may be able to obtain the same effect later by enlarging a section of the negative. **Above:** Pomp and ceremony makes for colourful snaps.*

CAMERAS

camera can be used in practice.

Any photographer over the age of about thirty has probably used an old-fashioned box camera, but many younger photographers would deny that they have ever done so. In fact, the 110 and 126 snapshot camera is the effective descendant of the old-fashioned box, with fixed focusing (relying on depth of field and a fairly uncritical user), a single aperture (something around f/8 – f/16), and a single shutter speed (often around 1/30).

The box camera has much to commend it. It is cheap, reliable, and easy to use. It is also very limited: it can only be used out of doors in good light. If you are prepared to restrict your photography to that extent, the basic box can be ideal. The better models can deliver quite acceptable pictures up to postcard size, though the results from some cheap 110 cameras could scarcely satisfy anyone. The cartridge loading of 110 and 126 cameras is certainly convenient, but for cheapness and good results, an old rollfilm box camera can equal almost any 110 or 126, and can be picked up in a garage sale or jumble sale for a tiny fraction of the price of a new camera.

At the top end of the box-camera market, the box camera shades into the compact camera, with built-in flash, perhaps some rudimentary form of focusing, even a zoom lens.

NON-REFLEX 35MM CAMERAS

Almost all popular, modern 35mm non-reflexes are of the 'compact' type and embody some form of exposure automation. Scale focusing is the norm, though some have coupled rangefinders and others are equipped with autofocus.

These cameras usually have lenses slightly shorter than the 50mm (2″) normally regarded as 'standard' on 35mm; this not only gets more in, but the inherently greater depth of field of a short-focus lens in practical use covers up errors in focusing.

Many have built-in flash: the use of flash generally is discussed in a later chapter.

35MM SLRs

These are discussed at greater length elsewhere; all that needs to be said here is that they are the most versatile and widely-used cameras amongst advanced amateurs and even professionals, and that the bottom-of-the-line automatic-only models such as the Nikon EM and Olympus OM-10 are easy to use and cost only a few pounds more than some compact rangefinder or non-SLR cameras. They accept most of the lenses and accessories available for their big brothers, and if you do decide to move up into the system they provide excellent second camera bodies.

INSTANT-PICTURE CAMERAS

The difference between these and all other cameras is, of course, their immediacy. The simplest of them are little more than box cameras, and even the most complex are only comparable with the average compact. Automatic exposure is usual, and automatic focusing is readily available – though with the long focus lenses necessary to cover the large film area, depth of field is limited and some form of focusing is all but essential.

Since they must accommodate a full-sized print, these cameras are necessarily bulky. The folding models, notably Polaroid's excellent SX-70 film version, are the most convenient; its reflex viewing and (on non-autofocus models) focusing, makes it easily the most versatile of instant-picture cameras.

The advantages, then, are simplicity and immediacy of results. The disadvantages are bulk (especially if you are carrying spare film packs) and the expense of the pictures. In fact, the price of prints is not too bad, bearing in mind the cost of processing and printing a conventional colour film, and the fact

Left: A tent in the back garden is the basis for an adventure. Stand by with camera to capture the expedition's more arduous moments as well as the rest periods, when rations are broken into. Long focus lenses will enable you to obtain candid shots. Above: Foreground interest has been retained by using the considerable depth of field of a wide angle lens.

Keystone XR 608. 110 cartridge load pocket camera,
f5.6 25-42mm zoom lens, fixed focus,
shutter 1/125-1/250, built-in electronic flash.

Far left: Having anticipated the route to be taken by the girl, the hopeful photographer secreted himself in the chosen spot. Focus and exposure were predetermined so that efforts could be concentrated on releasing the shutter when the subject came into view. An expression of joyful surprise was his just reward. Left: Fairgrounds, with their bright colours and happy atmosphere are yet another setting in which to picture the child. It is as well to choose a fast film, since this will enable you to freeze movement more effectively. For snaps such as this, follow the action with the camera, and take a number of exposures to increase your chances of success. Below: Children's appetites are invariably good on a picnic, and food that might otherwise be rejected will be eagerly devoured. This in itself is worth recording. Note the slight distortion of some of the foreground items caused by the use of a short focal-length lens.

Chinon 35 FA. 35mm compact camera, f2.8 38mm lens,
automatic focusing, automatic programmed exposure,
shutter 1/8-1/500, built-in electronic flash.

that there is less temptation to shoot a spare picture 'to be on the safe side', because you can see your results almost instantly.

Instant picture cameras are also very useful for making pictures to give people, far better than the usual unfulfilled promises to send them a copy when it has been processed back home on conventional film.

OTHER CAMERAS

Many people have an old camera somewhere, at the back of a drawer or cupboard, which they have been given, or have inherited, or whatever, and which is capable of very good results if only they could figure out how to use it. Typically, there are four kinds: old non-metered 35mm SLRs, old 35mm non-reflex cameras, rollfilm folders, and twin-lens reflexes.

The two 35mm types are reasonably well described elsewhere in this book, but the rollfilm folders and TLRs are not.

Rollfilm folders vary widely in sophistication, with the very best having top-flight lenses, fully speeded shutters, and coupled rangefinders. Before trying to use them, check that the bellows have no pinholes, that the front standard is not too wobbly when erected, and that the shutter actually works. Most will take 120 film; once again, an old-fashioned camera store or knowledge-able friend is your best ally. One piece of advice: when dealing with any unfamiliar camera, BE GENTLE. NEVER force anything: rather than something being stuck, it is far likelier that you are doing it wrong, and will break something. If it is jammed, and you want to try using it, take it to a repairer's (look in the yellow pages). Don't just take it to a dealer, unless it be our old friend the old-fashioned store.

In a dog-owning household, *no album would be complete without a series of snaps of man's best friend. The ease with which you will be able to immortalise Fido will depend on your patience, that of the animal, and his response to orders. An obedient pet will help matters no end. Little co-operation should be expected from puppies, and it may be worth employing the services of an assistant to keep it occupied whilst you manipulate the camera. Be professional and talk to your model throughout the session, but above all work quickly, as pressing engagements normally await it. A high camera angle as in the picture shown* **facing page top left** *will emphasise the dependence of a tiny puppy, or the haughty sophistication of the larger dog as shown* **top.** *Hounds, such as the Bassett shown* **left,** *can be pictured to effect at their own level, perhaps following a scent. Sometimes, formal portraits may be improved by using a prop as in* **facing page top right.**

GENERAL INFORMATION

The twin-lens reflex has already been mentioned in the section on viewfinders. These cameras are often capable of work of the very highest standard, comparable with a modern professional rollfilm SLR costing half as much as a small car. They are unfashionable, and some people find them awkward to use, but the results from (for example) the Rolleiflex, Minolta Autocord, Yashica 635 or Yashicamat are second to none. Get a friend or someone else to explain the camera to you, or buy a copy of one of the Rolleiflex or similar camera guides available from a number of publishers – they are still available. Most TLRs are similar enough to Rolleiflexes for a Rollei guide to be sufficient as an instruction book.

For all non-metered cameras, you will need either a meter or an exposure guide. Meters are not difficult to use, though details vary between models. Usually, you set the film speed (ASA or DIN) on the meter, aim the meter at the subject (pointing slightly downwards, so as not to include too much sky) and read the number against which the needle is resting. A calculator on the front of the meter enables you to work out the appropriate

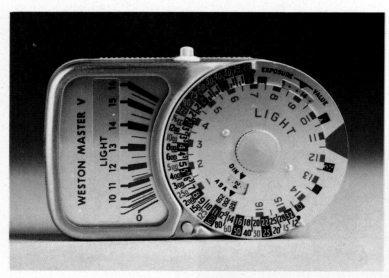

exposure. On the Weston V in the picture, for example, the needle is pointing to just over 11. Set the big red pointer on the scale of the calculator to the same number, and read off a choice of exposures from 1/1000 at f/3.5 to 1/50 at f/16 (or 1/25 at f/22 if your lens stops down that far).

Alternatively, use the following guides, which are given courtesy of Kodak:

ISO 100 (21°) ASA 100 (21 DIN)	KODACOLOR II Film			C135

Film price does not include processing.　　　　*Load/unload camera in subdued light.*
DAYLIGHT EXPOSURE: Cameras without exposure controls—take pictures in bright sunlight or hazy sunlight. **Cameras with adjustments**—determine exposure setting with an exposure meter set for ISO 100 (21°)/ASA 100 (21 DIN) or use the table below:

Bright or Hazy Sun on Light Sand or Snow	Bright or Hazy Sun (Distinct Shadows)	Weak Hazy Sun (Soft Shadows)	Cloudy Bright (No Shadows)	Cloudy Dull or Open Shade†
f/16　1/125s	*f/11　1/125s	f/8　1/125s	f/5.6　1/125s	f/4　1/125s

*f/5.6 for backlighted close-up subjects. †Subject shaded from sun but lighted by a large area of sky.

FLASH EXPOSURE: Use blue flashbulbs, flashcubes, or electronic flash. Divide flash guide number for ISO 100 (21°)/ASA 100 (21 DIN) by the flash-to-subject distance to determine the correct lens opening to use.
STORAGE: Store in a cool, dry, dark place. Have your films processed promptly after exposure.

Finally, before leaving the question of cameras behind, research has shown that many people regard loading anything other than a cartridge camera as being forbiddingly difficult. Admittedly it is possible to make mistakes, especially with 35mm

cameras, but if you follow the drill given below you will at least be independent of shop-assistants who may actually know very little about photography – and you will be able to stop pestering whoever usually loads your camera!

In the early days, loading films (or plates, as were used in those days) was simple and slow. Each plate was held in its own little box or plateholder, and each plateholder was loaded into the camera separately, exposed, then removed and replaced with the next.

Inevitably though, it is far quicker to use a roll of film with a number of <u>frames</u> or <u>exposures</u> in a row. Although this idea goes back to 1854 (using paper as the 'film'), it was George Eastman who really popularised the approach. In 1893 came the 'cartridge loading' Kodak, which the user could load and unload himself – earlier Kodaks were returned to the factory for loading – and since then there has been an endless search for ways to make loading simpler.

Nowadays, there are basically four systems.

The first is the rollfilm. Rollfilm uses black paper backing to protect the sensitive film. In use, the seal is broken and the spool placed in the camera. The end of the backing paper is shaped so that it can be attached to another spool (the takeup spool). After a turn on the winding handle, or knob, to make sure that the backing paper is firmly attached, close the back of the camera and wind on until the number 1 appears in the little window in the back of the camera. After exposing that one, wind on to 2, and so on.

***Above: A twin lens reflex with** semi-automatic frame counter, showing film start arrow aligned with the start marks on the camera. **Facing page top left:** 35mm camera showing cassette in position and film leader engaged in take-up* spool. ***Top right:** The film perforations should engage with the sprocket teeth on both sides before the camera back is closed and advanced to frame No.1. **Right:** A cartridge-load pocket instamatic with film in position.*

With modern, highly-sensitive films, be sure to cover the window with the little metal slide (or use a piece of black adhesive tape) when it is not in use. Some cameras have automatic frame spacing and even automatic first-frame positioning; this is covered in the handbook for the individual model, or can be explained to you by a knowledgeable friend or good camera dealer.

When you reach the last frame, keep on winding until the winding key suddenly feels free. Then open the back of the camera, fold the tip of the backing paper under, and lick-and-stick the seal which holds the roll shut. The film is now ready for processing, and you can transfer the old feed spool to become the new takeup spool.

The other common size (though rapidly dying) is 127, which is a smaller version of 120: the spools are about 1¾″ long instead of 2½″. You may also find 220, a professional long-loading version of 120 giving twice as many shots to a roll when used with a suitable camera, and 828 or 'Bantam', a tiny rollfilm made for long defunct Bantam cameras. Cameras requiring 116, 117, and other film loadings can no longer be used.

Rollfilm has been about since 1903 in its present form, and the 35mm cassette loading effectively dates from about 1925. The original Leica used a rather sophisticated self-opening cassette, but film manufacturers were quick to pack their film in disposable, thin metal, cardboard (now no longer available) and nowadays plastic cassettes.

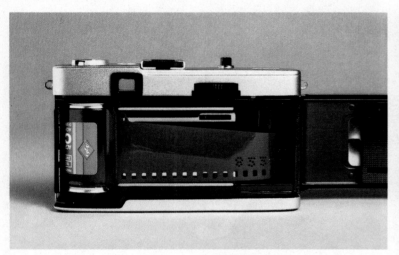

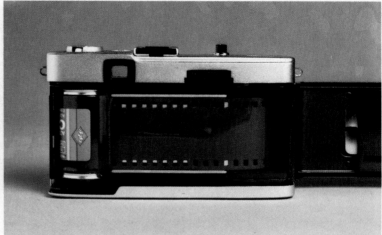

Although in the past there were many different kinds of roll-film, some giving pictures as big as 5 x 7″ on the negative, there are now only two in common use. By far the most usual is 120, which gives eight exposures 2¼ x 3¼″, ten exposures 2¼ x 2¾″ (only on a few professional cameras, which do not use the red window system), twelve exposures 2¼ x 2¼″, or fifteen or sixteen exposures 2¼ x 1⅝″. You can tell how many pictures your camera will give by measuring the film-gate with the back off; in any case, the window in the back will be so positioned that only the correct numbers (1-8 or 1-12) appear. If there are two windows on the <u>same</u> level they are used for 16-on loading: first you get 1 in the left hand window, then 1 in the right-hand window, then 2 in the left-hand, and so on. Any camera using this system will be very old now. If the two windows are on <u>different</u> levels, then the camera is a dual-format model, using a mask to change the negative size. One will show the 1-8 numbers, and the other the 1-12 numbers.

Once the camera back is *closed, keep an eye on the rewind knob as you wind-on to* *the next frame. If this turns, it indicates that film is correctly loaded.*

Despite the mystique which surrounds it, loading a 35mm cassette is quite easy. The cassette drops into the space provided in the camera – usually on the left as you look at the camera with the back off, but sometimes on the right. The lips, through which the film passes, are always uppermost and next to the film gate: it is not easy to load the film otherwise, but some people try!

The leader (the piece of film sticking out of the cassette) is attached to the takeup spool on the other side of the film gate. This is very much easier on some cameras than on others, and a few manufacturers (such as Canon and Konica) have simplified it considerably: you just lay the end of the film down near the take-up spool, close the back and wind on. Note that this is NOT available on all Canon and Konica models, and that attaching the film in the usual way is still necessary in many cases.

Operate the wind-on lever to make sure that the film really is securely fixed to the takeup spool: sometimes it can slip out, and although you <u>think</u> you are winding on, the film is not being transported through the camera. This results in a clear film with no image (when using negative film) or a black film with no image (when using slides).

Close the back of the camera and <u>lightly</u> tension the rewind knob, turning it in the direction of the arrow. Wind off the first two exposures, which will have been fogged whilst loading the camera, and are of no use anyway. The frame counter should now be at 0. Wind on again, and it will be at 1, ready for the first picture. As you wind on, the rewind knob will revolve, showing you that the film is being wound on: this is an old professional trick, as every photographer I know has at least once failed to load a camera properly.

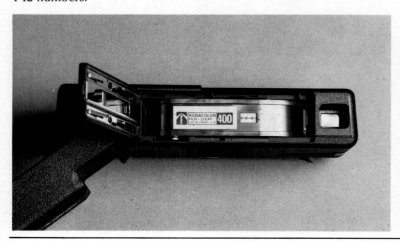

GENERAL INFORMATION

Wind on until you get to the frame-number at the end of the film: 12, or 20, or 24, or 36. DO NOT attempt to get another exposure out of the film: as often as not you will succeed, but you will also run the risk of pulling the end of the film off the feed spool so that it cannot be rewound. The camera will then need to be unloaded in a darkroom – and besides, there is always the likelihood that you will assume that you have rewound the film, open the back, and ruin the lot.

Rewinding is easy: press in a little button (or push a little lever on some cameras) and wind the film back into the cassette using the rewind knob or crank, turning it in the direction of the arrow. On some cameras, you have to keep the rewind button depressed all through the rewinding process; on others pressing it once at the beginning of the rewind is enough. The rewind button frees the sprocket wheel which transports the film: if this is not freed you will feel considerable resistance when you rewind the film. If you persist, you will tear and shred the film.

Some people rewind until they feel the little tug which signifies that the film leader is free from the takeup spool: the leader is then left protruding through the lips of the cassette to assist in light-sealing. Others rewind it all the way, so that there is no danger of re-using an already exposed film. If you like to leave the leader hanging out, then fold or tear it to show that the film is exposed – but do so carefully, as the additional strain on the cassette lips may itself cause them to part and admit light.

A few 35mm cameras use the obsolescent Agfa Rapid system of loading: once again, a good camera store will show you how this works. Agfa Rapid cassettes are shorter than the conventional variety, and are not rewound. They are not interchangeable with conventional cassettes except in a few very rare Alpa cameras.

The third loading system is the drop-in cartridge, either in 110 or 126 sizes. Whilst loading and unloading is very simple (they only go in one way) some people still try to force them. One of my friends, who owns a camera store, tells a very amusing story of a young man who reacted very angrily when it was suggested that they might load his camera for him. "What do you think I am, stupid?" he said, and then proceeded to load the cartridge in backwards. The sound of splintering plastic as he leaned on the back with all his weight to close it was alarming....

Seriously, if you line them up properly, these cartridges just drop in. Once they are in, wind on until '1' appears in the window; repeat until the end of the film. Continue to wind on until it says END or the backing paper runs out: as with rollfilm, there is no rewinding.

Loading instant-picture cameras is just as easy: once again, the cartridge will only go in one way. The procedure for removing the black protective cover varies between types, but if you follow the instructions packed with the film you will not go wrong. This, the fourth of the systems, is perhaps the easiest of all: when you run out of instant pictures, you just throw away the husk of the old cartridge and load a new one.

Whatever sort of camera loading you use, once you have got it right the first time you are unlikely ever to get it wrong again. If you like, get someone to show you how to do it – but in any case, do learn how to do it yourself. You'll never regret it.

With the exception of *weather-proof or underwater equipment, cameras will suffer irreparable damage if exposed to sand or sea-water. Wind-blown sand particles can enter the camera's smallest openings, quickly reducing it to a useless box, whereas salt-water will cause serious corrosion. When not in use, the camera should be kept in a polythene bag, away from the direct rays of the sun, as heat will affect the colour balance of the film.*

Mamiya U. 35mm compact camera, f2.8 35mm lens, symbol focusing, automatic programmed exposure, shutter 1/8-1/500, delayed action, built-in electronic flash.

FAULTS

The following information is reproduced by kind permission of Kodak Ltd from their Information Sheet AE-4(H) – *Better Pictures – next time!*

When you take pictures of your family and friends, your holidays and events, you'll want the best possible results. After all, these pictures are your mementos of happy times and special occasions. It's easy to take good pictures if you follow these few picture taking hints.

With a simple camera, outdoor pictures are best taken in bright or hazy sunlight. Where possible avoid having your subject partially in bright sunlight and partially in deep shade.

Keep the background as simple and uncluttered as possible.

Hold your camera steady. Squeeze the shutter gently to avoid moving the camera during exposure.

Hold the camera level. Use the horizon or vertical buildings as a guide and avoid side-ways tilt.

Encourage your subject to relax and act naturally. Pictures of people are better if they are engaged in some activity, rather than posed stiffly in a line.

Occasionally you may get a picture that is not as good as you hoped. We know the feeling – we've all suffered such disappointments from time to time. Next time it happens to you, look through the following descriptions and see if one of them fits your picture. We've tried to suggest reasons and remedies, so that you can try to avoid disappointment next time.

PROBLEM	POSSIBLE CAUSE	REMEDY
Bluish appearance	Colour film intended for use in tungsten lighting was used in daylight without a correcting filter.	*See the film instructions for filter recommendations or use in daylight film.*
	Distant or high altitude pictures were taken on daylight film but without a correcting filter.	*Use a UV filter over the lens.*
	Pictures were taken in overcast conditions or open shade.	*Use a 'Wratten' No. 1A filter or a haze filter.*
Reddish-orange appearance	Pictures were taken on colour film designed for daylight or blue flash but clear flash, photoflood or existing tungsten lighting was used.	*Use a blue flash, follow the filter recommendations or use a film designed for photoflood or tungsten illumination.*
	Pictures were taken on daylight film in early morning or late evening sunshine.	*Avoid taking pictures of people or any subject where correct colour is important, in the two hours immediately after sunrise and the two hours before sunset.*
Weak greenish or reddish appearance on colour pictures (may be mottled)	Film possibly outdated.	*Always check the expiry date on the film carton and ensure that you use the film before the stated date.*
	Film possibly stored where it was hot and humid.	*Store the film where it is cool and dry and have it processed promptly after exposure.*
Overlapping film	Film not advanced fully to the next picture or to the "lock" position.	*Ensure that you operate the winding mechanism properly until the locking position is attained.*
	Too many pictures taken on a roll.	*Check the number of exposures on a roll and keep a record with you. If your camera has an exposure counter, ensure that it is correctly set after loading the film.*
	Film winding mechanism in your camera needs adjusting.	*If in doubt, consult your local camera dealer.*
Black spots or black streaks	Dust, fibres or fragments of film inside the camera.	*Brush the inside of your camera with a sable-hair brush or blow it clean with a small rubber puffer.*
	The camera strap, front cover of the camera case or fingers in front of the camera lens.	*Ensure that there are no objects in front of the lens before taking a picture.*
Light streaks and spots	Direct rays of the sun or other bright light source shining on the camera lens. This generally causes bright spots and circles of light on the picture.	*Shield the lens from the direct rays of the sun. The shadow of your hand, held well outside the picture area, will do or position yourself so that the sun is behind a tree branch or other object.*
	Camera back opened before the film has been fully rewound to the end before unloading. This results in reddish-orange, light fogging creeping in from the edges of the film.	*Never open the camera back until the film has been completely wound to the end before removing for processing.*
	Film handled in bright daylight.	*Always handle in the shade when loading and unloading the film.*

Top left: With the sun behind *you, avoid casting your own shadow into the picture area.* **Top right:** *Shooting into the light without compensation will lead to such underexposure effects.* **Lower top right:** *Frame your subject well within the viewfinder to avoid such cut-off.* **Centre:** *Lack of subject sharpness due to incorrect focusing.* **Above:** *Camera straps, cases or fingers in front of the lens will obscure part of the picture.*

	Light leak in the camera. This results in light spots or squiggly light streaks on the picture.	*Seek the advice of your local camera dealer.*
	Extreme camera movement during exposure, due to the shutter sticking and staying open too long.	*The camera is in need of repair. Consult your camera dealer.*
Unsharp pictures – fuzzy images	Camera shake when the shutter was released.	*Hold the camera steady and gently squeeze the shutter release. For normal picture-taking be sure the camera shutter is not set for B (bulb), T (time) or L (long), if your camera has these settings.*
	Camera too close to the subject.	*Check that the focusing scale on the camera has been set for the correct subject distance.*
	Shutter speed not fast enough to stop the action.	*With an adjustable camera, use a high shutter speed such as 1/250 or 1/500 of a second for moving subjects. For a fast moving subject or where you cannot use a high shutter speed, follow the action by keeping the subject centred in your viewfinder. This is called 'panning.' Alternatively, change your position so that the action moves toward the camera.*
Foggy, misty pictures	This is caused by a dirty lens or filter.	*Clean the lens or filter with lens cleaning tissue or a clean, soft, lintless cloth.*
Slides too dark – prints dark and "muddy"	Insufficient light for taking pictures with a simple camera.	*See your camera instructions and the picture taking hints for outdoor photography.*
	Too high a film speed number used with an exposure meter or automatic camera with a film speed dial.	*Use the correct film speed as shown on the film instructions or film carton.*
	Lens opening too small, or shutter speed too fast (or both), for the existing lighting conditions.	*See the film instructions or exposure suggestions. See also under "Flash Pictures."*

FAULTS

Slides too light – prints "washed out" and contrasty	Obstruction over exposure meter window in your camera.	*Ensure that no object or shadow can obstruct light to the meter.*
	Too low a film speed number used with exposure meter or an automatic camera, with a film speed dial.	*Use the correct film speed as shown on the film instructions or film carton.*
	Lens opening too large, shutter speed too low (or a combination of both), for the lighting conditions.	*See the film instructions or exposure suggestions.*
Slides black – negatives clear. Due to lack of exposure	Camera shutter did not open.	*If in doubt, consult your camera dealer.*
	Film not properly loaded in the camera so that the film did not advance.	*Read your loading instructions carefully next time to avoid incorrect loading again.*
	Unexposed film sent for processing.	*Avoid confusing exposed with unexposed 35 mm film by rewinding it completely into the cassette after taking the last picture.*
	Lens cap not removed.	*Ensure that the lens is uncovered before attempting to take photographs.*
	Flash did not go off.	*See the camera instructions for taking flash pictures.*

FLASH PICTURES

Proper exposure is based on flash-to-subject distance. See the flash information on the flashholder, camera, film instructions or flashbulb carton. The details below give you additional information on possible problems and how to remedy them.

PROBLEM	POSSIBLE CAUSE	REMEDY
Flash failure on cameras that use flash-cubes or flashbulbs (not magicubes)	The flash did not function at all or went off too late. The most frequent cause is battery contacts that need cleaning or batteries that are weak or dead.	*To clean the battery ends and contacts in the camera or flash-holder, rub with a rough cloth. If they are difficult to reach, use a pencil with an eraser on the end to clean them. Always use live batteries and have them tested regularly, replacing when necessary. If the flash-cord has a screw-on adapter, ensure that it is tightened.*
	The flashbulb was faulty.	*Try another bulb.*

Top: A long exposure and camera movement due to a flimsy tripod, combined to create this slightly fuzzy shot. Centre: Subject movement and camera shake were responsible for this badly blurred picture. Such effects are particularly common in photographs taken on miniature cameras. Bottom: Many older cameras, especially those taking roll-film, have no double exposure prevention devices. Two pictures on one frame will result in such ghost images.

	The camera's flash mechanism is faulty.	*Consult your camera dealer and have your camera repaired, if necessary.*
Flash failure on cameras that accept magicubes	Faulty magicube.	*Try another one.*
	Camera's mechanism is in need of repair.	*Consult your camera dealer.*
Flash failure on cameras taking flip-flash	Faulty flipflash.	*If a bulb fails to flash, any remaining bulbs in that half of the flipflash won't flash. Turn the flipflash over and use the other half or install a new one.*
	Faulty camera.	*If the flash will still not function, your camera may be faulty. If in doubt take both the camera and any suspect flipflash to your dealer for advice.*
Flash pictures too light	Pictures taken too close to the subject with a simple camera.	*The typical distance range for a simple camera is 4 to 9 feet. See the camera instructions or the flashbulb carton.*
Flash pictures too dark	Pictures taken too far from the subject with a simple camera.	*See the camera instructions or the flashbulb carton for the correct distance to use.*
	Lens opening too small with an adjustable camera because flash-to-subject distance was underestimated or the wrong guide number was used.	*Use a range-finder or estimate the distance more accurately. See the film instructions or flashbulb carton for the proper guide number.*

	With an adjustable camera the wrong shutter speed or synchronization setting was used for your type of flash.	*Check your camera instructions.*
Glare spots	Shiny surfaces such as windows, mirrors, spectacles and even shiny woodwork will reflect the flash and cause glare spots in your pictures.	*To avoid these flash reflections stand at an angle to the shiny surface when you take the picture, instead of trying to take it head on.*
Red reflections in eyes, on colour pictures	Red or amber spots in the pupils of your subject's eyes are caused by reflection of the flash in the eyes.	*Use a magicube extender if your camera accepts magicubes or if possible, detach the flasholder to increase the distance between the flash and the camera lens. If neither method is possible, you can minimize the effect by turning on all the room lights, causing the subject's pupils to contract. This reduces the intensity of the reflected light that caused the redness in the pictures.*
Uneven exposure in flash pictures	Flash exposure depends on flash-to-subject distance. Therefore subjects at different distances in group photographs will appear lighter or darker depending on how far away they are from the flash.	*You'll get more even exposure if all subjects that appear in the picture are about the same distance from the flash.*

*Although blur can be used creatively to give a feeling of movement, this is generally not desired in family type snapshots. The picture **left,** shows how movement, together with a slow shutter speed, has rendered the children's features unrecognisable. The photograph **far left** was taken with the same degree of subject movement, but using a faster shutter speed to actually stop the action, and resulted in a satisfactory snap. Where light levels are low, faster films can be used to allow for a shorter exposure.*

Minolta 460 TX. 110 cartridge load camera
with 26mm and 43mm standard and telephoto lenses,
scale focusing, weather symbol exposure setting,
shutter 1/200, built-in electronic flash.

Regardless of the camera, the film, or the subject, there are various faults which crop up again and again in all snapshots. Broadly, they fall into three categories: equipment problems, subject problems, and lighting problems.

The traditional bugbears are poor focusing, poor framing, incorrect exposure, and camera shake. They are all very much more difficult to get wrong nowadays. In practice, the way in which they normally arise tends to be more a result of carelessness or hurriedness rather than an inability to use the camera. With a non-reflex camera it is very easy to forget to focus; the image in the viewfinder looks sharp, so we forget that the image on the film may not be.

Poor framing is rather less common, if only because modern viewfinders are so vastly superior to those fitted to the old box cameras and some rollfilm folders. Parallax problems, and cut-off heads, are the only ones which really remain. Users of the ghastly old 'brilliant' finders will remember not only the tiny and hard-to-see image, but the way in which the finder was often mounted on a flimsy metal bracket which was inclined to bend, so that the field of view of the finder and that of the lens only bore the most casual correspondence.

The usual reason for incorrect exposure is mis-setting the ASA dial on the camera's built-in meter. This is very easily done, and most (probably all) photographers have done it at some time. The easiest way to get around this problem is to standardise on one film – the ASA dial on the Nikon EM which is my

Simplicity of composition is an option that many photographers ignore, and yet, as can be seen, strong colours *and a high camera angle are the main elements that were combined to create this stunning series of pictures.*

favourite snapshot camera stays permanently at 400 ASA. On cameras where the meter reading has to be transferred manually to the camera settings it is again easy to forget: the only answer is to remind yourself before each picture. Some cameras use an 'EV' or 'LV' system, which combines the shutter speed and aperture into a single number – for example, EV 10 is the equivalent of 1/125 at f/2.8. It is also the equivalent of 1/250 at f/2, 1/60 at f/4, and so on down to 1/4 at f/16.

Camera shake can be minimised by holding the camera carefully and releasing the shutter gently, and by avoiding too-long shutter speeds which can be difficult with some automatic cameras, as already mentioned.

Whilst a fully automatic autofocus camera obviates most of these problems, some of them (such as setting the wrong film speed) can still arise, and others appear which would not affect an old-fashioned camera. For example, the batteries must be reasonably fresh, or both exposure and autofocus may be affected. Again, careless aiming of the autofocus patch may lead

BETTER SNAPSHOTS

Sports and action photography are generally the province of the fast shutter speed, however this should not discourage owners of the simple camera that may not offer this option. Panning, fast films, anticipation and even flash can be used to overcome deficiencies in equipment. Long lenses are frequently used in sports photography to fill the frame with the subject. It should be said however that these can make it rather difficult to follow the action, and will require greater precision in focusing. In the shots shown on this page, subjects were photographed at the peak of their action when motion was limited. **Facing page. Top:** *A fire barge shows off the power of its water cannon.* **Bottom:** *A moderate shutter speed was combined with a panning action so as to freeze the movement of the craft whilst still retaining an impression of speed in the blurred spray of the water.*

Olympus Trip 35. 35mm compact camera,
f2.8 40mm lens, symbol focusing,
automatic exposure, shutter 1/40-1/200.

to some totally inappropriate piece of foreground or background being the principal plane of focus, rather than the actual subject. Furthermore (and this applies to any auto-exposure camera), if the subject is rather out of the ordinary, the meter may be fooled and give the wrong exposure.

To take a simple example, consider a dark-skinned person against a white background. The meter is designed to integrate all scenes to a neutral grey. Because the white background dominates the picture, it will lead to a short exposure. Not only will the background be underexposed, but the person's face will be severely underexposed – and if you are using colour print film, remember that you are not dealing with <u>one</u> averaging meter, but with <u>two,</u> the one in the camera and the one in the automatic printing machine. If the background is brilliant in its own right, as might occur with a girl shot against a sunset, the girl will be reduced to a silhouette.

To compensate for this, many cameras have some form of override built in. On the Nikon EM, it is a simple button: pushing it in gives two stops extra exposure, enough to expose the foreground subject correctly at the expense of the background – in the case of the sunset, the girl might be correctly exposed, but the sunset would be quite washed out. A more sophisticated approach gives a choice of compensation factors, usually plus or minus two stops in half-stop increments.

The reverse case from the above – a light-skinned person against a black background – calls for compensation in the opposite direction. The automatic meter will tend to overexpose, so the subject will be completely washed out. This arises more rarely, but can happen (for example) when photographing fireworks at night.

BETTER SNAPSHOTS

If your camera has no compensation dial, one way to get around this is to use the ASA/DIN dial as an exposure compensation device. Doubling the ASA will halve the exposure: halving the ASA will double the exposure. Similarly, for one quarter of the exposure, multiply the ASA by four: for four times the exposure, divide it by four.

For altering exposure by less than one whole stop, either guess the appropriate ASA setting by eye, or use the DIN scale: each shift of a single DIN division represents ⅓ stop. Again, INCREASE the setting to DECREASE exposure, and vice versa.

Whether using the ASA dial or a built in compensation dial, be sure to return the ASA setting to its former value for more conventional subjects. A few cameras have a warning that the compensation is in use in the viewfinder, but the vast majority do not, and it is only too easy to be caught out.

This may sound strange, but it is easily illustrated. Consider the classic holiday snap, which shows Aunt Ethel against a tangle of ironwork, with a pavement artist in the foreground and a couple of onlookers at about the same distance as Aunt Ethel. The intention was to take Aunt Ethel against the Eiffel Tower, but the pavement artist was so interesting that he was included too. The Eiffel Tower is not really recognisable; the jumble of ironwork could have been the Brooklyn Bridge or the pier at

Below: Manhattan's skyline seen from beneath the Brooklyn Bridge. Below right: The Pan Am building dominates New York's Park Avenue, dwarfing the older facade of Grand Central Terminal. Buildings can be particularly effective in showing the character of a city. Modern architecture with its clean geometric lines of steel, stone and glass inevitably attracts attention and draws the eye heavenward. Specialist

cameras and empty streets are frequently used by professionals requiring a perfect representation, but the converging backward lean of the buildings pictured on the facing page is also effective. Reflections of clouds and adjacent structures will add interest.

Incidentally, it is impossible to 'hold' both the girl and the sunset on the same film: any film can only handle a certain brightness range, so if you expose for the highlights in a contrasty scene you will lose the shadows. Conversely, if you expose for the shadows, the highlights will 'burn out' to a feature-less white mass. With print film, a certain loss of highlights is not too bad, but with color slide (which has a very restricted brightness handling ability) the norm is to expose for the highlights and let the shadows take care of themselves. The only way to get around this is to use supplementary lighting, or reflectors, to shorten the brightness range – and this is dealt with at the end of this section.

The technical problems described above are comparatively easy to master – though that does not mean that you will never make such mistakes again! – and indeed do not exist for the majority of snapshot subjects using modern automatic cameras and colour negative film. Much more usual are the compositional problems which can arise even with perfectly exposed pictures.

Although these can take many forms, they all boil down to a single common fault: a failure to select what is important, and to separate it visually from what is not important.

Margate, so that has failed; Aunt Ethel is so far away that she might as well be one of the onlookers (if the photographer had waited, or even asked, they would have gone away); and the pavement artist, who might have some chance of being the principal subject, is lost in a jumble of other conflicting points of interest.

In fact, there are several pictures here. There is the Eiffel Tower itself, there is Aunt Ethel (who could be photographed at the pay kiosk, or by a sign if you want to establish where she is), there is the pavement artist (either in close up or in long shot, so that he relates to the Eiffel Tower) and if you want to expand it a bit there is the abstract tracery of the tower's ironwork against the sky, the reactions of the passers-by, the pavement artist's picture (and Aunt Ethel looking at it), the old woman in the pay kiosk collecting the money, and so on.

This leads us to the first golden rule: SIMPLIFY. Leave out everything you can. Move in close, so that you show the main subject clearly and obviously – in relation to the surroundings if you like – and eliminate everything extraneous. Be prepared to wait a few seconds whilst an onlooker gets out of the way, or to move a few feet or even a few yards to get a different viewpoint.

Ricoh AF-2. 35mm compact camera, f2.8 38mm lens, automatic focusing, automatic programmed exposure, shutter 1/30-1/250, automatic load, wind and rewind, delayed action, built-in electronic flash.

BETTER SNAPSHOTS

The second golden rule is really only a variation on the first. It is, WATCH THE BACKGROUND. The standard example is the tree growing out of the head, but it takes many forms: the GENT'S TOILET sign which you did not notice at the time but which now seems to occupy half the picture; the desert of waste paper and empty beer cans at the country resort; the confusion of jumbled lines behind the subject; the print dress which merges into the flowered background as effectively as camouflage.

There is no real way to avoid these pitfalls, apart from really <u>looking</u> before you take the picture. After a while, it becomes second nature to notice the lamp standards which ruin the mediaeval cityscape, the telephone cable that curves across the flawless sky, the No Parking signs screwed to the castle wall. It is best to look without using the camera viewfinder; this is particularly true of reflexes, where things which are comfortably out-of-focus on the viewing screen when the lens is wide open leap into distressingly sharp focus when it is stopped down to the taking aperture. If the camera has a depth-of-field preview button, which stops the lens down to the taking aperture whilst you are looking through it, use that. It will give you a whole new view of the subject!

Actually, the instant picture camera really comes into its own here, as you can see any disasters, which always seem to be more evident in the print than in real life, as and when they happen. Not only does this give you the option of reshooting, but the opportunity to compare the scene and the picture rapidly

Facing page: Light is influenced by the colours of the objects that reflect it. In this picture, a large yellow flower was used to provide a warm fill-in effect to the girl's face, as well as extra interest and femininity to the picture as a whole. **This page:** *Happy memories are what the snapshot photograph should attempt to capture. A well laid out album of such personal moments can become a chronicle of our family lives, a diary in which words are not required.*

sharpens your visual awareness. Many professionals have special instant-picture backs to fit to their rollfilm cameras, so that they can check composition, lighting, exposure, and so forth on the spot.

Since most of the rest of this book is devoted to ways of composing and arranging your subjects so that they stand out from the background and say what you want to say, there is not much point in saying more at this stage; but there are two things

BETTER SNAPSHOTS

worth bearing in mind before we go on. The first is that if you want to learn about pictures, the best thing to do is to study pictures. Look at the pictures in this book, which are captioned to help, and look at pictures everywhere else: in magazines and newspapers, on television, in advertisements, at exhibitions – everywhere. Try to analyse what you like and what you do not like, and do not be ashamed to try to copy the work that you admire: it is a very traditional way of learning. The second is that practice may not make perfect, but it surely does help. Take plenty of pictures, and criticise them yourself when you get the prints. Ask what went wrong, and how you could do it better next time. Throw out the rejects, or keep them as Ghastly Warnings, and show people only your best work. Your reputation will improve, your self-esteem will grow, and you will start living up to other people's (and your) expectations; and you will also find that whilst your percentage of rejects for technical reasons diminishes, your percentage of aesthetic successes grows.

Going on to lighting and its attendant difficulties, the first thing to consider is the colour 'balance' described earlier; the simple rule is that you cannot mix light sources in a single picture. Fortunately, there is an exception to this: electronic flash (and blue-dipped expendable flashbulbs) give the same colour of light as daylight.

Ricoh 35 FM. 35mm compact camera, f2.8 40mm lens,
symbol focusing, automatic exposure,
shutter 1/125.

This has two useful consequences: the first is that you can use flash <u>instead</u> of daylight, without changing films or using filters, and the second is that you can use flash <u>as well</u> as daylight.

When using any flashgun, remember that the effective exposure duration is the flash duration – which may be as little as 1/1000 second, or even less. Subject to minimum synchronisation speeds, it does not matter what shutter speed you use: the action-stopping ability will be the same. If, however, you use a very long exposure, say one second, either deliberately or because you have left the camera on 'auto' and it has decided that a long exposure is needed, you will get one of two interesting effects.

The first is that you may get an overexposed image – not <u>very</u> interesting – but the second is that you may get a 'blurred picture' <u>plus</u> a sharp image from the flash – which can be quite a fascinating effect.

The fact that many compacts have built-in flash can be both a blessing and a curse. It is a blessing because it means that you are never at a loss for flash when you need it, but it is a curse for three reasons. The first is that because it is there, it is often used whether it is needed or not: there are many circumstances where a fast film and available light would give a very much more pleasing and natural result. The second is that because the flash

*Facing page. **Top:** The floating gardens of Zochimilco in Mexico City are a popular spot with visitors. Gaily coloured punts such as these can be hired to travel the many intersecting canals, where photographers and flower sellers look for trade. **Bottom:** Singing Kenyan tribesmen create an unforgettable sight in their village setting. **Top left:** Although similar views of the Taj Mahal's symmetrical magnificence can be found in many books and postcards, these are no substitute for your own photograph, which will be a part of your personal experience. **Left:** Close-up detail of the fearsome dragon guarding the Jumbo Floating Restaurant in Aberdeen Harbour, Hong Kong. **Above:** Men and women separated by a fence during a religious ceremony at the Wailing Wall in Jerusalem.*

BETTER SNAPSHOTS

is so close to the camera lens, there is a danger of 'red-eye.' This occurs when the light from the flash is reflected back from the eyes of the subject, albeit coloured by the blood vessels in the eye; the result is that the subject looks like the Bride of Frankenstein. There is no way around this, except by ensuring that the subject looks slightly away from the lens, rather than directly at it, but the 'pop-up' flashguns fitted to so many compacts are, nevertheless, a step in the right direction.

The third problem is that built-in flashguns are seldom as powerful or as versatile as separate ones. The maximum power of a flashgun may be expressed in a number of ways, but a commonly used method is the guide number (GN). The guide number varies according to the film speed, but in use it is simply divided by the flash-to-subject distance to give the aperture needed. For example, a gun might have a GN of 33 at 100 ASA. If the subject is 3 metres away, then $33 \div 3 = 11$, so f/11 is the appropriate setting. Sometimes guide numbers are expressed for use with feet: for example, a gun whose GN was 33 (metres) at 100 ASA would have a GN of 100 (feet) at 100 ASA. It is customary to add (feet) or (metres) to published guide numbers: if they are not given, suspect the worst.

A typical add-on flashgun might well have a GN of 33 (metres), but a built-in one will seldom exceed 16 (metres); and as with apertures, the scale is not linear but according to a square law, so GN 16 (m) is about one quarter as powerful as GN 33 (m). To take a serious example, if the maximum aperture of the lens is f/2.8, then the maximum flash distance with the less powerful gun is just under 6 metres; with a GN of 12 (m), which is by no means unusual, it will only be just over 4 metres. The more powerful gun could manage nearly 12 metres at the same aperture!

Of course, most modern flashguns are automatic, and spare the user all such calculations. On many, the sensor for automation is fixed pointing forwards, so that even if you bounce the flash they still only read what returns from the subject. Others require that you open up a stop or so; the instructions with your flashgun should make this clear.

The latest innovation in flash for SLR cameras is the so-called 'dedicated' flashgun, which is made by the camera manufacturer to match a particular camera or range of cameras. These have additional contacts in the flash shoe which automatically set the shutter speed, and the flash power according to the lens aperture. A few models even read the flash through the lens of the camera, during exposure.

Whatever lighting you use, remember that light is the essence of photography. Each type has its uses: a harsh, glaring light can give drama to a picture, but would hardly be suitable for a delicate picture of a baby. Conversely, the soft delicate light of an overcast day might beautifully illuminate a child's features, but it would make a Mediterranean sun-spot look pretty gloomy: blazing sun would be more appropriate. As you get more practised, you will find more and more ways of using light – of playing with it, if you like – and you will find that this improves your own visual awareness and pleasure as well as your photography.

Top: Parascending is a sport in which only the intrepid will participate, however it can make for interesting snaps. Right: The growth in popularity of windsurfing means that such sights will be common at most waterside locations. Long lenses will generally be required to get a meaningful picture. A UV filter will help avoid the hazy effect from which these pictures sometimes suffer. *Facing page: Pleasing snapshots such as these result from a keen eye rather than a bag-full of equipment.*

Minolta Weathermatic A. 110 cartridge load, f3.5 26mm lens, symbol focusing and exposure adjustment, shutter 1/200, built-in electronic flash. Waterproof down to a depth of 5 meters.

HOLIDAYS

One of the nicest things about holiday snapshots is that they remind us of things we think we had forgotten. A good holiday snap can trigger off a cascade of memories, best shared with someone else, so that it becomes "And do you remember . . ." . . . "Yes, and what about . . ." To a limited extent, we re-live the holiday – and, assuming that we enjoyed it, we re-experience the pleasure we had during the holiday.

Whilst it is true that a picture does not need to be very good to have this effect, there is equally no denying that a comprehensive and clear set of pictures can conjure up far more than half a dozen out-of-focus and barely distinguishable prints. This is even more true if we are showing the pictures to someone else; it is much more enjoyable and less embarrassing for both parties if we do not have to keep up a running commentary of the order of, ". . . and that's Peter, but you can't see him very clearly because the camera moved and anyway the lady with the big hat got in the way and . . ."

This does not mean that we should only take photographs for other people, of course. Looking through my own holiday pictures I find dozens of things which are important to me – the bicycle I rode in Spain, for instance, or the Land-Rover based bus which was used to cope with the appalling roads and utter lack of maintenance – but which someone else might find deadly boring.

Top: The water droplets of a breaking wave are frozen in mid air by the action of a fast shutter. Left: On interchangeable lens 35mm cameras, focal lengths of around 85mm are ideal for head and shoulders shots. A cheap alternative is to combine your standard lens with a x2 converter. Here, a high angle has enabled the blue of the water to serve as a plain background, and a wide aperture ensures that interest is concentrated on the face. Above: For shots like this, avoid using wide lenses close to the subject, the effect is not flattering. Facing page. Top left: Attract the child's attention when all camera settings have been made otherwise the smile may disappear. Top right and bottom: The passing years bring new interests.

Praktica MTL3. 35mm single lens reflex,
taking all 42mm screw thread lenses.
TTL stop down metering, manual exposure,
shutter 1-1/1000, delayed action.

HOLIDAYS

After all, who is interested in a rather tired-looking bicycle leaning against a brick wall? I am – but I do not expect anyone else to be.

For most people, a large part of the pleasure of a holiday is the anticipation and planning, though this should not be allowed to assume such proportions that the holiday itself is a disappointment! The planning should extend to the photography, too.

First, NEVER EVER take a new and untried camera with you. This is one of the oldest pieces of advice in the book, but still it is repeatedly ignored. The people who are hit hardest by this are the ones who are going on the holiday of a lifetime – an American on a European tour is the classic (and saddest) example, though I have known it happen to Englishmen going to Africa and Frenchmen on a world cruise – and who buy a new camera because they feel that the old one is not good enough. They shoot several dozen rolls of film, and when they get home they have them processed, only to discover that the meter was malfunctioning, or the lens was not stopping down properly, or the shutter was only part opening, or any one of a hundred other faults. The faults need not be mechanical, either: a mistake in the handling of the camera can be enough.

If you buy a new camera, leave yourself plenty of time to test it. Ideally, put a roll of Kodachrome slide film through it: Kodachrome repays correct exposure with some of the finest rendition available, but its latitude is comparatively small and errors in exposure will be shown up. If the camera can expose Kodachrome correctly, it will have no difficulty with colour print film. At the very least, put a roll of 100 ASA print film through – a 12-exposure cassette will be enough–to check that it is in working order. You will need to allow a week for processing (three weeks if you use Kodachrome), a couple of weeks to argue with the dealer/importer/manufacturer if things go wrong, and the same again to test a replacement; if that one goes wrong too, you are either (a) using the wrong camera or (b) plain unlucky – you may care to take it as an omen and cancel the vacation!

When choosing a new camera, remember that there is no need to go mad and buy the latest super all-singing all-dancing SLR. In the first place, a simple camera is sufficient for around 90% of all holiday snaps, and a basic compact will extend this to something around 99%. Secondly, it will take you a while to feel at home with a new and complex camera. It is far better to buy the new camera as long before the holiday as possible, so that you can see if your new role as ace photographer really suits you. Surprisingly often, people buy a marvellous new camera for a vacation – and then end up using it less than the old one (because it is too much trouble) and getting worse results (because they do not understand it).

Take plenty of film with you, because in most holiday resorts film is overpriced and may not have been stored too well. In some places, you will be unable to get your favourite films. The same goes for batteries – and incidentally, when did you last change the batteries in your camera? – and for flashbulbs if you still use them. Unless you have a vast excess, you should have no trouble at customs, but a good way to ensure this is to take the outerwrappings off the film and mark the inner wrappings clearly with the film type. Carried like this, even a dozen or two dozen rolls will seldom excite any comment.

Rather more of a problem can be the X-ray machines at airports. Regardless of assurances to the contrary, at least some of these can and do damage film. The best way to avoid trouble is to carry the film on your person, in pockets. The next best is to ask for a physical search; most people will respond to a polite request, though there are some customs men who refuse. Failing that, pray. The lead-lined bags sold to protect film are useful in

Ricoh A-2. 35mm compact camera, f2.8 35mm lens,
symbol focusing, programmed automatic exposure,
shutter 1/30-1/250, delayed action,
built-in film winder.

Taking lots of snaps of the same scene from different viewpoints will undoubtedly increase your chances of getting a satisfactory shot, but unless you are a keen photographer, there really is no need. Look around and see what you find attractive, then think how these features could be brought into the picture. The process needn't take more than a few seconds. The picture shown **left** was given added interest by showing the cloud formations contrasted against a deep blue sky, whilst a palm tree adds a touch of texture and exotic colour. Don't restrict your shots simply to eye-level scenes, a better picture may be had from above or below. **Below:** when showing the horizon, make sure that it retains a natural look by keeping the camera absolutely level, and crouch down if you want it to appear higher up in the picture. **Facing page:** Acapulco's luxury hotels and fantastic swimming pools make it a dream holiday location.

HOLIDAYS

this respect. If your camera is reasonably expensive and reasonably new, it is worth carrying receipts for it and any accessories so that you do not get charged duty on the way home; hardly anyone worries about tourists arriving. In some countries, though, the serial numbers of cameras and accessories are entered on your passport, and if you cannot produce the same items on leaving the country you will have problems.

Once you actually arrive and start taking photographs the holiday has really begun – though few people would go as far as a friend of mine, who says that he would not go on holiday if he could not take his camera!

The ground rules are as laid out in the last chapter; select, simplify, and watch out for those backgrounds. One thing you do <u>not</u> have to do is to shoot with the sun behind you; this may have been the case in the bad old days but now all you are likely to get is screwed-up eyes as the person you are photographing squints against the glare. Remember, though, to increase exposure if you are shooting into the light, unless you want the subject in the foreground to turn out under-exposed.

Happily, the days when the camera was brought out only for the summer holidays and special occasions are long-gone. Flexible equipment and materials mean that pictures can be easily taken all the year round. Whether on holiday, or simply showing children at play, there can be no shortage of subjects that will reflect the exuberance that the winter season brings, as the pictures on these pages show. The colours of nature may be subdued at this time of year, but those of modern winter clothes are frequently vibrant and will stand out well against the snow in the blinding light of a sunny day. Having used the camera outdoors on a cold day, don't be surprised to find the lens misted over with condensation on returning to a warm room.
Facing page: *A fast shutter speed was required to 'freeze' the snow, kicked up by holiday-makers.*

Ricoh 35 EFL. 35mm compact camera f3.8 40mm lens, scale focusing, semi-automatic exposure, shutter 1/125, built-in electronic flash.

The choice of subjects is up to you, but you may find that it is worth doing a bit of planning beforehand to decide what you want to photograph. A good way to do this is to buy (or borrow) a picture-book about the place in question; or, of course, if you have already been there before, you can work out what characterises the place for you and what you would like to photograph. I would suggest a threefold division, into the landmarks, the local colour, and the personal memories.

The landmarks are the 'musts,' the Statue of Liberty, the Arc de Triomphe, Trafalgar Square, the Ginza, the Mannekin Pis. They are all available in picture postcards, but there is something inherently nicer about the pictures you have shot yourself. Furthermore, your own pictures can have you in them – this should not make any rational difference, but it does. You can also try to get pictures which are different from the standard views – have you ever seen a picture of the Taj Mahal plus its surroundings, for instance? The landmarks are the easiest to plan, and in a sequence of pictures can form what film makers call 'establishing shots' – if this is the Eiffel Tower, we must be in Paris.

On the other hand, you may decide to ignore the landmarks altogether; I have no picture of the Arc de Triomphe, or the Bois de Boulogne, to remind me of visits to Paris, nor have I pictures of Picadilly Circus or the Houses of Parliament to remind me of London – but if I were planning a coherent set of pictures I should probably shoot some.

Local colour is what you cannot wholly appreciate until you visit a place. In Paris, there are all sorts of examples: people carrying loaves of bread, patisseries advertising croissants chauds a 4 heures, political posters and graffiti, the entrances to the Metro, old-fashioned fishmongers selling oysters and coquilles, even the beautiful filles de joie around the Strasbourg St-Denis area if you are prepared to risk photographing them.

In much of Eastern Europe and Africa, it is forbidden to photograph military installations. This does not seem too unreasonable until you discover that it includes the airport at which you landed . . . the railway station . . . road bridges . . . military (and police) personnel . . . government offices . . . More than one plane- or train-spotter has found himself in very hot

HOLIDAYS

Hanimex 35S. 35mm compact camera, f4 38mm lens, fixed focus, fixed exposure, shutter 1/125, built-in electronic flash.

*Before embarking on a holiday, it is as well to be aware of the landmarks that you will wish to see and photograph. A short stay can so easily be spoilt by the indecision that results from ignorance and insufficient planning. Do not, however, limit your snaps only to the better known views, and try to observe the colour of the everyday life. Photographs of this will later help you to re-live the experience. **Left:** The Dome of the Rock dominates Jerusalem's Old City skyline, the magnificent turquoise, gold and white of the arabesque designs are even more imposing when seen close-up. **Below left:** The life-style of Hong Kong's boat people changes little with the years. **Below:** A horse-drawn carriage pictured against Rome's 137 Spanish Steps, where artists show their latest works. **Facing page. Top left:** The fishing fleet moored in the harbour of picturesque East Neuk, Scotland. **Top right:** Feeding the pigeons in St Mark's square, Venice. This incredible city, intersected by 150 canals and rich in art and architecture, offers the visitor and photographer more sights than possibly any other, anywhere in the world. **Below:** Montmartre is the hub of artistic life in Paris, still preserving much of its village type atmosphere.*

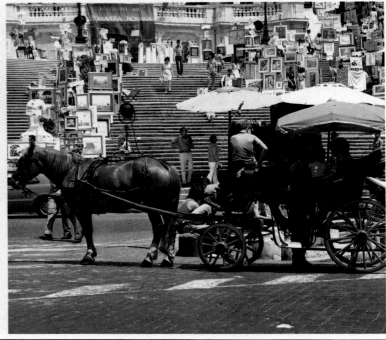

HOLIDAYS

water. On the other hand, most of the paranoid governments which impose such rules are desperate for foreign currency, which means that they have to put up with the tourists who bring it, so unless you are very careless you run little or no risk.

Personal memories are the subjects which are special to you. For example, you might want to photograph the hotel or villa where you stayed; the bar where you drank; the pool where you swam. It need not be so obvious, either. If you enjoyed a particularly good meal at a little <u>bistro</u>, then photograph it – with the proprietor outside, if you can persuade him. Whenever you look at the picture, you will be reminded of the food and hospitality. Again, if you sat and argued politics with someone you know you will never see again, sitting at a pavement cafe, photograph them. Photograph the shop where you bought the Scottish lambswool sweater; photograph the shop where you did <u>not</u> buy the incredibly beautiful diamond ring; photograph the beach where you swam, and the beach guard who was always chatting up the girls; photograph the girls themselves . . . whatever you photograph, do not stint the film. Even if you throw away half of it when you come back, you will still have a set of pictures to remember the holiday by.

Whilst you are on holiday, you will need to take some care of your equipment. Storing the film in a cool place – as cool as you can find – is an obvious precaution. If you have an expensive camera, theft is a risk – in Rome, for some reason one of the worst places for this sort of crime, scooter-riding bandits may snatch a camera from your shoulder, so wear it securely around your neck. Insurance is an excellent idea, against both theft and accidental damage. Whilst you are not using the camera, either leave it with the hotel's security staff (only worth while with more expensive cameras) or hide it under a pile of dirty underwear, which one traveller assures me has protected his camera in the past.

It is a good idea between films to check the operation of the camera. Check the shutter and the film transport mechanism, and use a blower brush to clear out hairs, film chips, etc. before reloading.

If your camera is kept in the cupboard between holidays, make sure that it is in good working order before your departure. Check that shutter and meter are operating correctly either by shooting a test film or asking your local dealer to look it over. Thoroughly familiarise yourself with any new equipment, and replace any old batteries, as these can fail without warning. A lens hood and skylight filter will be useful in sunny climes, helping image quality and protecting the lens. Keep all films away from heat and damp as these will affect the colour of your pictures, and have them processed by a reputable laboratory as soon as possible. It is worth re-stating the dangers that sand and seawater pose to your camera's mechanism.

Konica C35 EF. 35mm compact camera,
f2.8 38mm lens, symbol focusing,
automatic exposure, shutter 1/60-1/250, delayed action,
built-in electronic flash.

Processing abroad is seldom a good idea, for two reasons. The first is that it only requires a slight delay for you to lose your film entirely, and explaining where to post it, or that you are going on Friday, or whatever, is bad enough in English: in Spanish or Greek it can be impossible. The second is that some processing labs at holiday resorts (in any country) are run by get-rich-quick merchants, who may well deliver abysmal quality. And once again, complaining is both difficult and time-consuming. Instead, wait until you get home, and take the pictures along to your usual processor.

Once you have your pictures, edit them. Throw out (or at least remove) the technically poor ones, and the ones which duplicate each other. Have the courage of your own convictions: pick the ones you like, rather than giving the lot to someone else and asking them to do it. Put them into sequence, especially if you were shooting colour slides and are planning a slide show. Few things are worse than a random selection of slides, a few in Disneyland, then some of the Golden Gate, then Yosemite, then back to Disneyland, then someone you met at a party, then the airport, and finally 'this is us setting off.' At the end of it all, you will not only have something you can show to someone else: you will have something which will mean a lot more to you, too.

CHILDREN

Apart from holidays, children probably account for the expenditure of more film than any other subject. They are so fascinating to their parents – especially if they are the first – that the temptation is to photograph their every movement. Subject to practical limitations – the cost of the film, and the need to live as normal a life as possible whilst raising the children – the best way to react to this temptation is to take Oscar Wilde's advice, and yield to it. I have never yet met a parent who regretted a single frame exposed of their child, and the more comprehensive the record of the child's growing up, the more precious it becomes in later years. Do not, however, expect other people to be as entranced as you are. Here, more than anywhere else, you are shooting for yourself and your immediate family. Before showing a single picture to anyone else, edit ruthlessly. Select a single picture that best shows your child; if you must, and you really can winnow no further, select two or three or even half a dozen, but NO MORE.

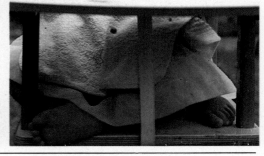

To many, photography may hold little fascination, yet, consider how much poorer life would be without the humble snapshot. Imagine having no record of your child's early years; its total dependence, its first steps, the smiles and tears. All these would be consigned to your past, vague memories of days gone by.

Ricoh 35 EFS. 35mm compact camera, f2.8 40mm lens, symbol focusing, automatic exposure, shutter 1/125, delayed action, built-in electronic flash.

When photographing children, *try to show them as they really are rather than as you would like others to see them. The latter approach rarely works. Natural looking snaps are invariably more successful than those resulting from the forced modelling session. Long lenses and an abundance of patience are useful, as they will enable you to follow the child at a distance, recording their vast range of moods and expressions as they engage in their activities. Be prepared to waste some film getting the desired shot as they are unlikely to sit still for any length of time.*

CHILDREN

*Upright for figures and oblong for landscapes are very general rules that are worth bearing in mind. The decision may be based on a pose or background view, or your personal sense of balance and composition. Don't be afraid to "cut off" parts of the subject in gaining the desired effect. **Left:** Semi-impressionist splashes of colour were provided by the flowers in the foreground softened by the shallow depth of a long focus lens. A fuzzy background, with pleasant areas of light and dark, avoids distraction. **Above:** Swings are a particularly useful prop in child photography in that they keep the subject in place and can almost ensure a balanced pose. **Facing page. Top left:** A slow shutter speed was used to show movement in the outstretched hand, and makes the subject's focus of attention obvious. **Top right:** Although formerly frowned upon, shooting into the light is not bad practice, and can lead to very pleasing results. Take care to measure light off your subject or increase exposure by around two stops. This can be done by lowering the ASA on cameras that permit no other adjustment. **Bottom left:** A touch of feminine grace is added to the shot by the hand raised to the hair. **Right:** A long lens focused on the dog gave a pleasingly soft look to the ship's captain.*

Hanimex 35 Micro Flash. 35mm compact camera, f2.8 32mm lens, symbol focusing, symbol exposure setting, shutter 1/60-1/180, built-in electronic flash.

CHILDREN

Helios 110A. 110 cartridge load, f4 20.5mm lens, fixed focus, fixed exposure, shutter 1/125 & 1/250, built-in motor wind and electronic flash.

You can slant your choice of picture towards the audience, of course. If you are showing it to parents with children of similar ages, they might love a picture of your daughter covered in chocolate or ice-cream; but your more fastidious (and childless) friends might find the same picture merely revolting, and resolve never to invite you to their place until the child is of a more respectable age.

Whilst almost anything may be regarded as fair game when photographing your children, remember that children are human. They have feelings, just as you do, and something which appears funny or cute to you may appear quite embarrassing or even humiliating to a child; this is all the more true of the teenager, but even surprisingly young children are very much aware of their own dignity. If the child has been used to a camera being about from the earliest days, then you can get away with more than someone who introduces the camera later; but sooner or later the crunch will come.

Even pictures which the child does not mind at the time may embarrass it later, especially if you persist in showing your pictures to all and sundry. Whilst a certain amount of embarrassment is an essential part of growing up, it behoves any

parent to exercise a bit of restraint at times. During the most difficult period – the early to mid teens – it may be as well to 'lose' certain pictures altogether, and rediscover them when the child is old enough to appreciate them.

From the point of view of equipment, children are extremely demanding. They move about unconscionably quickly, darting from light to shade, and in and out of focus, until it can seem almost impossible to catch them. A simple fixed-focus camera is likely to prove awfully limiting, not least because small children are very small and really demand close-ups for good pictures. The addition of a flashgun will improve matters immensely, and fast film permits small lens openings or faster shutter speeds (without flash) or both. The ideal camera is probably a compact with a bright viewfinder and a 35mm lens, though a reflex must run it a close second.

Whatever the age of the child, you should <u>always</u> get down to its level. Quite apart from the psychological implications of 'looking down' on someone, we have all seen the craned neck and upcast eyes which look so unnatural: photographing a child at its own eye level, or even from below, makes for a much more interesting and original picture. The effect is even worse if you

Facing page: Don't try to force a smile out of children for every snap you take of them. They too have a serious side to their natures that is worth showing, and the results can be equally pleasing. With two children who are generally deadly rivals, you will probably have to resort to threats or bribery to elicit such a temporary show of affection. Left: Bright light directly overhead together with a dark background were combined to show hair texture in both the girl and the dog, adding an extra sparkle to the picture. Above: Windows and various other openings can provide an eye catching frame for your subject.

CHILDREN

use a wide-angle lens, because the child's head (already large in proportion to its body by adult standards) looms even larger, and the disquieting and unflattering image is that of a tadpole. For relatively static children, the waist-level finder of the twin lens reflex is ideal, but the laterally reversed image makes action following difficult. Because the techniques vary so much according to the age of the child, the rest of this chapter is devoted to the different categories, by age.

BABIES

Except to their parents, most very small babies tend to look similar. Until they learn to crawl, they are fairly inert and difficult to photograph: the classic picture, of the nude baby in the middle of a rug, is an excellent illustration of this. Furthermore, even the most jovial baby never seems to smile for the camera (it is rumoured that those who do make a fortune from babyfood commercials). An invariably successful photograph is that of mother and baby together.

Crawling babies move astonishingly quickly, rather like piglets. They also have a wider range of expressions, and can quite often be cajoled into a smile. A time-honoured but effective trick is to have an assistant jingle some keys; this will often draw the baby's attention, and with any luck elicit a smile as well. The assistant should be down on the baby's level, too – which usually means hands and knees.

Like adults, some babies look better than others in the nude. The mere fact that the child does not object is irrelevant: after all, it has limited means for objection at its disposal. Always consider very carefully whether you really want a picture of a baby in the nude, and make it a conscious decision rather than a mere following of fashion. You may also wish to consider unconventional pictures – bath time, changing time, etc. – rather than the accepted playing-in-the-garden, playing-with-the-cat poses. These are, after all, the times when it is most especially your baby, rather than just another baby in a garden.

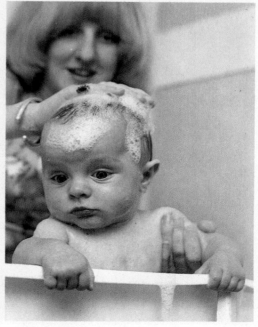

Konica Autoreflex TC. 35mm single lens reflex,
taking full range of Konica fit lenses.
Shutter priority automatic exposure with full manual override.
Shutter 1/8-1/1000, delayed action.

Facing page: The arrival of a new baby alters the life-style of any family, where it instantly becomes the centre of interest and attention. The snapshots that we take are an expression of the love and fascination that we feel. They can be used to record even those events that others may consider mundane.
This page: *The unique properties of photography enable us to chart the growth and development of our children, the joys of which can later be re-lived.*

TODDLERS

Toddlers present much the same problems (photographically) as babies, but they are very much more people in their own right: their faces are beginning to develop character, the range of expressions and emotions is much wider, and the range of activities is very much greater.

Once again, you may choose to photograph bath time, even potty time (though this is one of the pictures it is best to 'lose' during the child's teens). As the child begins to develop individual interests – playing with favourite toys, or fighting with the neighbours' children – you will also find that this provides a rich source of photographs. There are, however, times when he or she does not feel like being photographed, and you can be in for a battle of wills. My own inclination is to give in – after all, I don't submit to being photographed if I don't want to – but sometimes a picture can be irresistible.

It is worth going along with the child's inclinations to a considerable extent. For instance, some children love dressing up: others hate it, and are happiest in their oldest clothes. Why try to change that? If you can spare some old cosmetics, lots of little girls love to try making up 'like mummy'. Again, if a little boy likes playing with guns, forget the pacifism for a while –

CHILDREN

Left: When shooting indoors, avoid using flash as a matter of course, available light can give a particularly pleasing result. **Bottom left:** A low angle may not be normal in showing people but sometimes it is the only way to get rid of, or introduce a particular background. **Below:** Avoid red-eye in flash photographs by holding the gun away from the camera, or ask the subject to look away from you. Harsh shadows can be avoided by bouncing the light off walls or ceilings, or by using reflectors. **Facing page:** Close-up shots taken in bright sunlight risk being spoilt by shadows appearing on the face. Select your subject's position to minimise these, or use a reflector to throw light onto the face. A piece of white card is usually sufficient, and as shown, can add a lively sparkle when seen reflected in the eyes.

Keystone Everflash 3570. 35mm compact camera, f5.6 38mm lens, fixed focus, fixed exposure, shutter 1/125, built-in electronic flash.

CHILDREN

photograph him hiding in the undergrowth, the deadly soldier in ambush. Make the photography part of the game (you can play at being a war correspondent – but toddler armies are vicious, and often shoot their own war correspondents!)

CHILDREN 5-11

With children of this age, you are often dealing with miniature adults. Children can be very grave and serious if they want to – so why not try a very formal picture, seated in a large armchair? They enjoy going out for the day – so photograph them with their noses pressed against the glass in the reptile house of the zoo, or trying their luck at the fairground. They like dressing up and pulling faces – so photograph that. Once again, try to get involved in their world.

If they like your photographs, they will want to be photographed. If you make a big production out of it, insisting that they wash their hands and faces, they will not. If you waste their time, they will not like it: when you are in the middle of an urgent game of cowboys and indians, a five-minute break to have your photograph taken can be a welcome break (if it is fun) or interminable (if it is not).

You can often trade the photographs you want to take against the photographs they want taken. If you want your daughter immaculately scrubbed and dressed for her grandmother, trade that for a picture taken the way she sees herself (which is quite likely to vary enormously from day to day). If it means a picture of her standing on her hands with her tongue out, then take it – and I'd lay bets which will be the more interesting picture, and which one you will both (or all three) value more in years to come.

There are many different ways in which children can be portrayed, and the techniques you use – the way you frame the subject, the depth of field you show, depend entirely on you and the effect you prefer. In order to choose, however, you must be aware of the options available and how to use them. With this knowledge, you should find that the photography itself becomes more creative and enjoyable.

Olympus OM10. 35mm single lens reflex taking full range of Olympus fit lenses. Aperture priority automatic exposure, shutter 2-1/1000. Accepts dedicated flash, motor wind and manual exposure adapter.

TEENAGERS

From about twelve or so, the teens set in with a vengeance. Hitherto sweet-tempered children become unpredictable; extroverts become shy; shy boys become aggressive; and any mood or attitude can change to any other at any instant.

Nevertheless, if you treat the average teenager with the same courtesy as you would an adult, you will not do too badly. The difficulty lies in not being patronising, in attempting to be 'one of the gang'. You are <u>not</u> one of the gang (not if they are your children, anyway), and the best you can hope for is to remain on good terms. For about three or four years, my father and I maintained a sort of Mandarin truce, each speaking politely to the other but always somewhat distanced: then, when I was about seventeen or eighteen, I began to come out of it. Before that time, he was not a real person – not in the same sense as other people, anyway: he was (as fathers tend to be) an omnipotent and omniscient figure. After that, I began to appreciate him as a person, very kind and likeable, generous and knowledgeable in many fields.

The reason for this little bit of autobiography is just to remind you how you felt about your parents at the same age, and that your children are now adjusting to you in the same way. It may seem to you that this involves exaggerated respect for a young whipper-snapper; but if you want to get the pictures, respect is the key.

For the best results, and the fewest hassles, try to photograph your son/daughter whilst they are doing things that interest them; hobbies, say, or sports, or sitting reading, or dancing. Do not try to intrude in groups, but suggest in private that you would quite like to photograph him with his friends, or her with her boyfriend. Let the idea ferment for a while; you may be surprised.

The other possibility is to let your children take the photographs themselves. Lend your son the camera, with a roll of film, and tell him that you would like a couple of good pictures of him, but he can use the rest of the film as he thinks fit. To be sure, it will cost you the price of the developing and printing – but it may also get you the picture you want.

PERSONAL MOMENTS

Holidays are not the only times we want souvenirs; and children are not the only people we want to photograph. There are all kinds of other occasions which we want to record, such as weddings, christenings, birthdays, graduation days, sports days, days out . . . the list is all but endless. Sometimes we want the pictures to remind us of the happy times, and on other occasions it is a sort of dogged determination to chronicle the event if only to prove that we lived through it.

Such occasions can be roughly divided into five categories. The first are the formal ones – weddings, christenings, barmitzvahs, graduation days, and so forth. The second includes the domestic occasions which may be no less important to us, but lack the formal structure of the first type. Examples include birthdays, Christmas, Thanksgiving, the new car, and the garden in bloom. The third category is for those activities which normally involve a non-family group; club outings, church festivals, etc. The fourth group is Days Out – days at the seaside, at the zoo, at Christmas illuminations. The last group is Public Occasions – big

events in the life of the community or even the nation, which you want to photograph.

Inevitably there is a lot of overlap, and (for example) Guy Fawkes night, or the Fourth of July, may be either a domestic occasion or a group activity, or possibly even a day out; but by mixing the techniques described in the different sections, we shall get the effects we want.

Faced with a camera, *extrovert children surrounded by their peers are likely to put on a show, as can be seen in the photograph of milkoholics* ***below.*** *Classroom scenes such as those shown on these pages may not be a subject available to many, but they help* *demonstrate the type of snaps that can be taken of groups of children.* ***Facing page:*** *Bright sunlight streaming through the windows provided natural highlights and strong shadows that add mood to the pictures, in each case spotlighting the central character.*

Zenit TTL. 35mm single lens reflex, f2 55mm lens, TTL stop down metering, manual exposure, delayed action. Accepts 42mm screw mount lenses. Shutter 1/30-1/500.

PERSONAL MOMENTS

FORMAL OCCASIONS

Many of these correspond to what anthropologists call <u>rites of passage,</u> ceremonies which mark our transition from one accepted social status to another. For example, first communion, barmitzvah and batmitzvah, and the ceremonies by which primitive tribes declare a boy to be a warrior all have essentially the same effect: they separate (to a greater or lesser extent) childhood and adulthood. A christening admits a child to the body of the Church; a wedding publicises a couple's commitment to one another.

Consequently, these ceremonies are usually centred around a specific person or people – the bride and groom, the first communicants, the new graduates, or whatever – and our first impulse is to photograph them.

Whilst it is usual to have professional photographers along to many of these occasions, there is no doubt that all too often their work falls into stereotyped forms. Sometimes this is fine: after all, the main purpose of a wedding group is to provide a recognisable record of those present, and we do not look for great art in the composition. At other times, though, the results are disastrous. We have all seen those first communion pictures, in which an unfortunate girl is posed like a Victorian chromo-lithograph of a saint, clutching her rosary or some other suitably pious prop and staring into the distance. Far better to have her laughing with the priest, or kneeling at the altar, expressing what really happened instead of some preconceived nonsense which is exactly the same as every other communicant processed by the same photographer.

The same applies to all the other occasions: the graduate standing self-consciously in gown and mortarboard, degree in hand; the barmitzvah boy, always (for some unfathomable reason) photographed against a black background; the wedding couple, imprisoned by a trick of photographic montage in a brandy glass; they are all clichés, and even if we want to have them as a formal record of a formal occasion, the candid picture is far more revealing, and far more interesting.

This is where the snapshotter has the advantage over the hired professional. First, his pictures do not <u>have</u> to come out, so the whole thing is more carefree. Secondly, they do not <u>have</u> to cover certain specific occasions – the signing of the register, the cutting of the cake, and so on, and because the amateur has more time, he can afford to try for the more interesting pictures. Furthermore, because he is an invited guest instead of a hired hand, he can afford to take a bit more of a risk. If the professional photographed the bride's mother looking a bit tipsy, or the best man pinching a bridesmaid's bottom, it might be ill received, but if a friend or member of the family does it then it is likely to be the source of considerable amusement.

Official wedding photographs *are best left to the professionals. Although their services are often expensive, they are usually experienced in covering such events and are more likely to produce good pictures of such an important occasion. The lack of personal involvement leaves them free to concentrate on photography and their ability to manage crowds is an art most of us lack.*

Polaroid 640. 600 instant-print film, fixed focus lens, automatic programmed exposure, shutter 1/3-1/200, automatically activated electronic flash assistance for all exposures.

There is of course no reason why you should not take your own snaps to supplement the professionally taken photographs. Indeed, yours may show a warmer and more personal approach that comes of familiarity. Conceivably, they will even be better. If the professional has been commissioned to cover only the ceremony, you could concentrate on showing before and after scenes at the bride's house or

reception. If it is a church wedding, check with the priest as to whether flash, or even photography, is permitted during the ceremony. Observe the photographer and learn from him, but do not interfere with his work or follow him around copying his every shot. Take snaps of the moments that the professional may ignore. In that way, you will have a more complete record of the happy occasion, rather than a duplicate set of photographs.

PERSONAL MOMENTS

These little sideshows are often the best pictures from a formal occasion; you should never neglect the parents and grandparents, the nieces and nephews, the pages and bridesmaids, the bride's and groom's friends, and so on. The only trouble is that you may become so fascinated by their antics that you quite forget to photograph the pincipal players! Never neglect the humour of a situation, either; a photograph of the happy couple, surrounded by half a dozen identical electric toasters, is well worth having.

Inevitably, the type of pictures which you will be able to take may be limited by your equipment. If you have a simple box camera, then you will be limited to outdoor shots – though surprisingly often, you can get fascinating informal pictures even so. Flash may sometimes be inappropriate; it is invariably inappropriate during church services, for example, though opinions (among clergy and laity) are divided on whether photography of any sort should be permitted during an actual service. In practice, many clergymen are prepared to re-stage such things as the putting-on of the ring, or the christening itself, for photographs. If you are in doubt about photography, or about the use of flash, a quiet word beforehand with the people concerned will often be enough to clarify matters.

DOMESTIC OCCASIONS

Some of these may centre around individuals – the birthday girl, or the boy with his first motorcycle – but many are family occasions, when everyone is equally involved. The big danger lies in forgetting this, and concentrating (usually) on the children. To be sure, Christmas and Halloween and so forth loom much larger

Above: Watch the child's face on Christmas morning, it will reflect the joy and surprise of this long-awaited event. **Top right:** *A high camera angle was needed to show both boy and ornamental pond beyond.* **Right:** *A big brother's restraining hand is sometimes necessary in getting a snap.* **Facing page. Top left, right and bottom:** *Pictures of the children enjoying their summertime pursuits in the nude are fine, but avoid them unnecessary embarrassment by not exhibiting the snaps indiscriminately in later years.* **Top centre:** *Simple, attractive shots such as this are an integral part of any family album. Do not ignore the obvious.*

Minolta Pocket 470. 110 cartridge load pocket camera,
f3.5 26mm lens, symbol focusing,
automatic programmed exposure, shutter 2-1/1000.

PERSONAL MOMENTS

in a child's life than in an adult's, but this does not mean that they are not important to adults too. I remember one family Christmas where watching my 25-year-old sister-in-law unwrapping her presents was every bit as rewarding as watching my eighteen-month-old nephew unwrapping his; the pure delight on both their faces was wonderful to watch.

Some domestic occasions are inherently outdoor, and others indoor. Outdoor ones are easy to photograph with any camera, and include such things as the new family car, or the garden in bloom. It may seem a bit strange and self-indulgent to photograph the new car, but why not do it? It is quite an important part of most people's lives, and one well worth recording.

Indoor occasions are rather more difficult. For some things, such as unwrapping the presents on Christmas morning, flash is about the only practicable approach. Use bounce flash if you can, or even try moving a couple of bright table-lamps in close and using 400 ASA film without flash. If you have an f/2.8 lens, and a shutter which can reach 1/30, you should be able to do this.

At parties, even professionals give up and resort to flash. It is possible to get pictures without, but it requires ultra-fast lenses (f/1.4 or faster) and 'pushed' film rated at twice or four times the usual speeds – a service not often available in amateur labs. The important thing is to make sure that you fill the frame with something interesting; even at the liveliest party, it is all too easy to end up with a picture which seems to consist mostly of floor and wall, with two rather bored-looking people talking to one another.

GROUP ACTIVITIES

We belong to some groups willy-nilly: few of us, for example, have much say regarding the schools we attend. Others, such as offices and other workplaces, are voluntary in the sense that we choose to work there, but only partially voluntary in that we might not choose those people as friends despite the fact that we go on a works outing with them, or to an office party. Yet other groups we belong to because we really want to – the local church, for example, or a sports club. And a fourth category is

Fujica STX-I. 35mm single lens reflex, f1.8 50mm interchangeable Fujica bayonet lens, TTL metering, manual exposure, shutter ½-1/700, delayed action.

To obtain satisfactory results indoors without flash, you will have to position your subjects thoughtfully, in order to make the most of the available light. When photographing children, it is unreasonable to expect them to stand still for any length of time, so light levels must be adequate to enable a blur-avoiding shutter speed to be selected. Fast films and lenses are useful, but because of their cost, the latter may not be practical. Artificial room lighting can be used to assist the natural light levels, and this is likely to give a warm yellowish cast to your photographs, which you may find acceptable. **Left:** A wide variety of expressions can be observed during such absorbing games of chance. The light reflected by the board helped to retain detail in the children's faces. **Below:** The sunlight streaming through the church window enabled the photographer to freeze this moment of vocal endeavour during a choir practice session.

Facing page: Children's parties are colourful, exciting events that are ideal for taking snaps. Here, the photographer has captured the entire group of revellers. It is worth taking several shots from all sides, so that all the participants are recorded. **Above:** The family gathering may be a common occurence, nevertheless, you won't regret having pictured it. A tastefully arranged table such as here, is best shown from above with a wide angle lens.

PERSONAL MOMENTS

dedicated purely to enjoyment – the social club, or even the informal group of friends.

Whatever the group, there are two big differences from the family. The first is that we do not know the people as well as we know our own immediate family – indeed, we may hardly know some of them at all. The second is that we are not usually on home ground, in our own houses: we are usually out and about with them.

The camera can help us to get to know them better. Most people are delighted (if slightly embarrassed) to see pictures of themselves, and as long as we avoid taking overtly embarrassing pictures such as Mr. A making a pass at Mrs. B, we can expect our efforts to be well received.

As with parties, though, the difficulty lies in capturing the spirit of the occasion. The usual rules apply – get in close, and beware of distracting backgrounds – but there are a number of other techniques for getting the photography thoroughly into the swing of things. For example, it is often a good idea to do a 'set piece' at the beginning, one of those rather self-consciously posed group pictures with everyone in it. This gets them used to the idea that the camera is about, as well as being fun in its own right, both to take and to look at later. If you do set a picture up, though, be sure to work quickly – people <u>hate</u> having their time wasted when they would rather be enjoying themselves.

Flash can be a positive advantage, instead of being (as it usually is) a drawback. It makes people realise that they are being photographed, encouraging a certain amount of extrovert behaviour and freeing inhibitions – if people believe that they <u>ought</u> to be having a good time, they generally see to it that they <u>do</u>.

It is sometimes a temptation to 'hide behind the camera,' and photograph the action without joining in; this has a number of drawbacks, including the fact that unless you get into the spirit of the thing you may be unable to capture that spirit, and the risk of breeding resentment amongst your subjects who see you as a snooper instead of a fellow. On the other hand, serious drinking will not do your ability to manipulate the camera any good!

It is always a good idea to show people the pictures as soon as possible, while the event is still fresh in their memories. If they

Chinon CM 4s. 35mm single lens reflex, taking K-mount range of lenses. TTL metering, manual exposure, shutter 1-1/1000, delayed action.

*A number of snapshots of the occasion will make the thrills of a fun-filled day at the fairground all the more memorable. Fast films, with their inbred latitude, are ideal if you wish to continue shooting after dark, and they will help you freeze the frenzied pace of many of the amusements. Static shots, as shown on the facing page **left** and **top right,** will be simple to take and are the perfect record pictures, but try to convey some of the excitement as well. A long lens and a sense of timing helped catch the fear-filled expressions of the riders **facing page bottom,** on the roller-coaster. **Left:** The yellow glow of the lights on the dodgem track is typical of daylight film exposed to artificial light. **Below:** This evocative blur was achieved by using flash in conditions where the light levels were already quite high. The flash freezes the movement, whereas the slow shutter captures the blur of the action.*

PERSONAL MOMENTS

ask for copies, make sure that they realise how much this will cost – it can be extremely annoying to end up several pounds out of pocket because people do not actually pay for pictures which you thought that they had ordered. There is a great advantage in becoming known as the person who takes the photographs, both because it gets easier each time you do it and because it usually makes you popular and ensures that you are remembered when invitations are being handed out! If people never see the pictures, on the other hand, they will wonder why not – and as people always tend to think the worst, this is guaranteed to make you unpopular.

DAYS OUT

A day out can be any one (or more) of a hundred things: a day at the seaside, a day visiting some historic monument or national park; a day at the races; or even a day out shopping.

Much of what has been said above is applicable, as is the advice given on vacation photography. Usually, a compact

Don't consign all your snaps to the obscurity of an album. If you have one that particularly appeals to you, have it enlarged.

The bigger print invariably looks more imposing, and framed and hung on the wall it will give you endless pleasure.

Konica C35 EFP. 35mm compact camera,
f4 38mm fixed focus lens,
fixed exposure with underexposure warning,
shutter 1/125, built-in electronic flash.

PERSONAL MOMENTS

Pentax Auto 110. Cartridge load single lens reflex, taking Pentax 110 interchangeable lenses, automatic programmed exposure, shutter 1-1/750, dedicated flash and film winder.

camera is ideal: it is small, light, doesn't get in the way, and produces a totally reliable picture when used out of doors in good light. At night, out of doors, matters are a bit different. Flash is usually useless, unless you are photographing people very close, and although you can try using the 'B' setting on your shutter there is a severe risk of camera shake unless you use a tripod or other firm camera support. Quite a lot of subjects are surprisingly bright though, and if your camera has a reasonably fast lens and a fair range of shutter speeds you can often photograph things like Christmas illuminations by their own light.

The biggest difficulty you are likely to have is getting the processing lab to print things properly: their automatic machines are unlikely to be able to cope with the large areas of black which are inevitably involved, and will try to lighten them. The result is likely to be an unpleasant greenish-black background with washed-out highlights. It is as well to ask your dealer to write BLACK BACKGROUND in the little box on the processing envelope provided for special instructions: at least it strengthens your case when you return the pictures for reprinting. Alternatively, use colour slides for the best effects.

Top and facing page top: Back views such as these allow the photographer to concentrate on the overall composition of the snap while still providing a telling picture. Facing page bottom: A pool of light in a woodland setting was used to obtain pleasant highlights on the crouching girl. Left: Delicate clothes were chosen to blend with the countryside setting and the stile helped bring both subjects to the same level. Above: The older child may resent the interruption of a game, the expressions of distaste making for amusing snaps.

PERSONAL MOMENTS

PUBLIC OCCASIONS

Getting good photographs of great occasions – Papal and royal visits, parades, even the opening of a shopping centre by a celebrity – is difficult. For a start, crowds get in your way and obscure your view. You are likely to be a long way from the principal actors, both for practical reasons – there is just not enough room for everyone to be as near as they would like – and nowadays, sadly, for security reasons.

Press photographers have two advantages. They are usually given privileged points of view, either close in or high up, so that no-one obscures their view, and they are equipped with all manner of expensive cameras and long-focus lenses to enable them to get a good sharp picture no matter how far away they may be. It is by no means unusual for a press photographer to have the price of a car around his neck in cameras, motordrives, and lenses; and unless you are very rich or very dedicated, you are unlikely to be able to match this.

What you can do, though, is try to get a good viewpoint. It may be that you know someone who owns a house, or works in an office, along the parade's route. If not, you could always ask someone – people are often amazingly accommodating about such matters, and if you get your request in first (before they get tired of being asked) you stand a good chance of getting the viewpoint you want.

Alternatively, you can reconnoitre the route beforehand, pick a good spot, and get to it <u>early</u>. This may be a bit of a nuisance, but it is standard practice among press photographers to be in place by 5 a.m. for something which starts at eleven!

Unless you do have a very good viewpoint, or a telephoto lens, you have very little chance of getting a close-up picture of the celebrity in question. What you can capture, though, is the spirit of the whole thing: the crowds around you, the pomp and colour of the parade, the sheer numbers in the massed bands, and so forth.

There are two main ways of doing this. The first is to choose a good vantage point, but fairly well back – somewhere that affords a good view, but is further back than most people are likely to think of, at least at first. From there, you can shoot over

the heads of the crowds so as to show both the crowd and the event. The other is to get in with the crowd, as close as you can, and hold the camera up high over your head to take the pictures. You will not be able to use the viewfinder, of course, but with the slightly wide-angle lenses fitted to most compacts and simple cameras this should not be too important. Focusing is by scale and guesswork, and the tilted angle and rather arbitrary framing will add to the immediacy of the picture rather than detracting from it. Usually, just holding the camera at arm's length will do, but some people go further and attach them to walking sticks using rubber bands and masking tape. Some even go so far as to make up periscopes to allow reasonable precision in aiming the camera, and there is at least one periscope attachment which allows users of SLR cameras to focus and compose with the camera held a foot above their heads.

One trouble with shooting crowds is that they do not <u>look</u> crowded in the pictures: there may have been ten thousand present, but the picture shows mainly empty pavement. There are two ways to counter this effect, which is caused simply by the limited field of view of the camera. The first is to shoot from a

viewpoint one or two feet above people's heads, as described above – a sea of heads always looks more impressive than an array of backs – and the other is to take reasonable care that there are, in fact, plenty of people in the direction that you are photographing. Merely because they are packed in like sardines in some places does not mean that they will not be a bit thin on the ground in others!

Because of the difficulties involved in taking pictures 'live,' at the event, many choose instead to take them from the television screen. Whilst it is impossible to make hard-and-fast exposure recommendations, because televisions vary so much in brightness, the following guidelines may be useful.

First, you do NOT need flash. The TV screen is providing the light itself: if you fire a flashgun, all you are doing is lighting up the glass on the front of the screen and the TV set's surroundings,

Amusement parks, adventure parks and playgrounds are happy hunting grounds for the snapshotter and an exciting world of makebelieve for the child. Observe the antics from a distance if you want natural candid shots, and make full use of the bright colours that surround you. Pictures left and facing page © Walt Disney Productions.

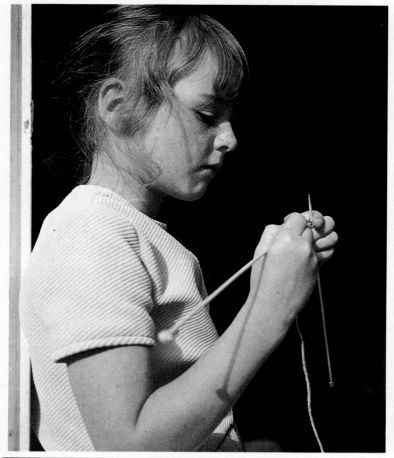

Minolta Hi-matic G2. 35mm compact camera,
f2.8 38mm lens, symbol/scale focusing,
programmed automatic exposure, shutter 1/60-1/250.

and the resulting picture will be far worse than if you had not used a flashgun.

Secondly, a TV image is traced out by a rapidly-moving spot, which scans the screen at mains frequency (50 times a second in the UK, 60 times in the US). Shorter exposures than 1/25 sec. (1/30 in the US) will not, therefore, give a full image; but substantially longer ones may well show more than a single image. The exposure must, therefore, be 1/15 or 1/30 second – even in the United Kingdom, 1/30 will give enough of the picture in most cases, and many simple cameras will not allow 1/15 to be selected. Metering is usually straightforward, in that a reading of the whole screen will give the correct exposure.

Thirdly, framing may be difficult; if your camera focuses close enough, you may still have trouble with parallax (the error caused by the difference in viewpoints between the camera's lens and the viewfinder): use parallax correction marks if supplied, or guess as best you can. If in doubt, leave a small margin around the screen.

Fourthly, do not expect superb image quality. Many of the pictures you see which are apparently taken from a TV screen are complete fakes, and others are heavily retouched. The light from a TV set is very blue, and whilst this can be filtered out to a certain extent during printing, colours may not look very natural.

Finally, remember that copyright subsists in the image, and that you are technically likely to be breaking the law by recording it. Whilst this will rarely lead to any trouble if the pictures are taken for your own private use, if you make any attempt to publish them or show them to a wider audience than your family and friends you may find that the television company objects – assuming, of course, that it gets to hear about it.

Facing page. Top left:
Shooting almost into the sun tends to weaken colours, leading to a softer, flatter look. Although formerly discouraged, such techniques are worth trying in your search for the better snapshot. **Top right:** *Backlit subjects against a dark background stand out particu-*

larly well. The water in the bird-bath was here used as a reflector, illuminating the face, which would otherwise have lacked detail. **Bottom left:** *The unlit interior of a room can be especially effective as a backdrop in shots where all attention is meant to be focused on the subject.* **Bottom right:** *The direction of the light can influence the appearance of textures considerably.* **Above:** *The disappointment of an empty net.* **Right:** *A loudhailer, cap and binoculars transform a little girl into a tyrannical sea captain. A standard lens was used at wide aperture to avoid showing the distracting background.*

ACTION PHOTOGRAPHY

Action photography is one of the most difficult subjects to tackle without specialised equipment. By definition, your subjects are usually moving, so you need the action-stopping effect of a fast shutter speed. Furthermore, you are usually at some distance from the action – though there are some sports where you can get frighteningly close – and unless you have a long-focus or telephoto lens you are likely to get a depressingly small image in the middle of the picture. This is made worse by the wider-than-usual lenses supplied on many compacts.

In practice, this limitation is so severe that unless you can get nearer the action you might as well give up for many subjects: you have only to think of those hopefuls up in the back row at Wimbledon or the World Series who fire off their 110 cameras (complete with flash – which is effective for all of ten feet!) in an attempt to capture their idols' exploits.

Of course, if you cannot get near the action, it is always worth considering photographing the spectators. The elation as his side scores; the depression when the other side saves a goal; either can make a worthwhile picture of a football fan. This does not only apply at a major sporting event, either: have you ever watched a mother urging her child on at a kindergarten foot-race?

If you can get close enough, there are a few basic techniques which are generally applicable. The first, and most important, is panning or following the action. Suppose you are photographing a racing car. Get it in your viewfinder, and follow it. When it fills the viewfinder, press the button – but be sure to follow the movement through, or you will have a jerky and blurred image. Obviously, you will not have time to set speed and

The most successful sports photographers are generally specialists who are familiar with the particular events that they are covering. It is sound advice therefore to learn the basics of the activity before you begin to photograph it. Without this knowledge, anticipation is all but impossible, meaning that the best shots will pass you by. The professional's standard equipment is generally a motorised camera fitted with a long lens and mounted on a tripod. However, these are not essential and good general shots of the field of play, as shown on these pages, can be taken with the ordinary fixed lens camera. It is as well,

however, to use a fast film in case you need to select fast shutter speeds or if the light is low.

aperture, or to focus, so have everything set up beforehand, even down to the extent of prefocusing the camera on the spot in the road where you intend to press the shutter.

This technique, which can be applied to anything moving in a predictable course from athletes to airplanes, allows you to use a surprisingly low shutter speed because the relative movement of the camera and the subject is not great. For example, it might take a 1/2000 second shutter speed to halt a speeding car – but with panning, a speed of 1/30 might be enough. The background will also be blurred, which adds still further to the impression of speed.

In fact, a low shutter speed, with a certain amount of blur, can give a better impression of speed than an action-stopping 1/2000. The effect can be enhanced by making use of 'compound movement' – the way in which parts of the subject move very

Yashica ME 1. 35mm compact camera, f2.8 38mm lens, symbol focusing, aperture priority automatic exposure, shutter 1/60-1/360, delayed action.

It may be that the sport, rather than photography, is your main interest, the latter simply a convenient means of recording the interesting moves or moments. This being so, you will already have a good knowledge of the event, and indeed you may be a participant with a privileged viewpoint. **Facing page. Left:** Opposing school teams form a line-out in a game of rugby. **Top:** The contemplative, relaxed nature of a game of bowls requires no knowledge of action techniques. **Centre:** American football is a spectacular and extremely physical sport that is particularly photogenic. **Bottom:** The set-pieces in a game of soccer are the ideal time to take a snapshot. **Left:** Cricket is a peculiarly English summer sport that often looks more leisurely than it is. Close-ups can lead to great action shots. **Below:** Windsurfing is the newest of the Olympic sports.

ACTION PHOTOGRAPHY

Minolta SRT 100X. 35mm single lens reflex,
taking Minolta fit range of lenses.
TTL metering, manual exposure, shutter 1-1/1000.

much faster than the whole. For example, a sprinter may hit 15 m.p.h., easily arrested with a 1/30 second shutter speed when panning – but his legs and arms will be moving a lot faster (as well as in a different direction, up and down) and may well record as a blur. The same applies to a horse's hooves or the wheels of a racing car.

One phenomenon of which you must be aware when panning (or indeed any sort of action photography) rejoices in the name temporal parallax. Put simply, this is the result of the difference between the time you press the button and the time the camera's shutter goes off – it is named by analogy with viewfinder parallax, which is a result of the different viewpoints of the viewfinder and the camera lens.

The smallest delay you can expect is of the order of 1/60 second. This would apply to a non-automated non-reflex camera. After this, it depends on how much has to happen before the shutter fires. At worst, on an auto-exposure autofocus camera, both the exposure and the focus have to be set by the camera after the button is pressed; about 1/10 second delay is by no means unusual, and a slightly wheezy autofocus can just about double this. For illustration, a car travelling at 100 m.p.h. travels nearly 35 feet in 1/10 second!

A second technique makes use of the 'dead moment', based on the old law that what goes up must come down. For example, at the peak of his jump, a pole-vaulter is moving surprisingly slowly, and quite a low shutter speed is sufficient to 'freeze' the movement – though once again, compound movement can add enough blur to suggest the action.

This technique can be applied to a surprising number of sports: the catcher jumping for a ball, the footballer heading the ball, even the steeplechaser going across a jump (though here you would need to combine it with panning).

Yet a third approach is to concentrate on the beginning or ending of an event. The concentration on a runner's face as he waits on the starting blocks; a strong man preparing for the jerk; the discus thrower preparing for the throw; the landing of the long-jumper (watch out for flying sand); the hammer-thrower or golfer as they watch the flight of their respective projectiles through the air.

You can extend this to include the preparations and aftermath of an event: the mechanics working on the racing motorcycles in the pits, or the muddy team trooping off the pitch. Photograph the starter, pistol in hand; the timekeeper, with his stopwatch; the coach, on the bench.

Apart from that, there are various specific techniques which apply to individual types of event. Some of these are described below in no particular order. In order to get good pictures of any of them, though, you will need three things. The first is a good eye for composition. The second is a knowledge of what you are photographing: for sports, it helps if you either play them yourself or follow them closely, and for circuses, theatres, etc., it helps if you are familiar with the programme or play – it is best to see it beforehand if at all possible. The third is luck – bonne chance!

Privileged positions and long lenses are a great help in getting the best sports action shots. Zoom lenses are ideal as regards composition, especially when you are forced to stay in one place. On their longer settings, these generally need to be mounted on tripods or steadied against firm objects.

Stunning, explosive action shots can be obtained by varying their focal length during exposure but this technique requires practice. If possible, survey the setting before the event to find the most advantageous spot. Certain events will enable you to pre-focus on a point where action is bound to occur.

ACTION PHOTOGRAPHY

FOOTBALL, BASEBALL, CRICKET, LACROSSE

These, and a number of other sports, are chiefly distinguished by the fact that they range over a great deal of ground. It is also impossible to venture onto that ground, so that without telephoto lenses it is going to be difficult to get any details unless the players happen to be very near you.

General shots of the field will be just that – mostly field, and hardly any players. There are a few places you may get good pictures – close to the goal mouth, for example, or during a line-out – but in general you would do better to concentrate on the spectators. This will be the only practicable approach at professional games where you cannot actually stand on the touchline.

GYMNASTICS, FENCING, JUDO, KARATE

There are several indoor sports which are restricted to comparatively small areas; the ultimate is gymnastics using fixed equipment (horses, etc.) where you can pre-focus on the equipment. With the parallel bars, the subject is even more static.

By contrast, fencers move up and down the p<u>iste</u> alarmingly rapidly, and the best pictures always seem to take place out of shot. Nevertheless, if you watch closely for the first part of the assault, you can detect a certain personal preference for one part of the piste – some fencers always advance, others always retreat, and a third category likes to stay in the middle.

In any case, you are going to need the fastest film you can get and a fast lens: if your camera can manage no more than

The colourful characters, their daring acrobatics and total dedication, make the true skateboard enthusiast and his sport superb snapshot material. The drab concrete surface of the track means that you will have to concentrate on the people and the action. Unless you are a participant, or are known to the competitors, ask for permission to take photographs; it will invariably lead to a greater degree of co-operation. During the runs, watch the critical or admiring expressions of the knowledgeable observers as well as the skyward leaps, abrupt turns, natural balance and occasional falls of the competitor. Avoid getting too close to the action in this or any other sport: it can be distracting and dangerous.

The unpredictable *flamboyance of a skateboarder's performance can make action following difficult. Choose your viewpoint and wait for the subject to enter your viewfinder. Quick reflexes, a fast shutter speed and if possible a small aperture should help you get a sharp picture. Head on action, or that diagonal to your field of view, is generally easier to capture than movement crossing your finder, and will enable you to use slower shutter speeds in avoiding a blurred picture. In such cases longer lenses can be used without difficulty, to give interesting close-ups of the subject.*

ACTION PHOTOGRAPHY

f/2.8 you may not stand much of a chance. DO NOT use flash – it can be very distracting to the participants, and the temporary blind spot it causes can make the difference between winning and losing.

BASKET BALL, SQUASH, JAI ALAI

These are rather like the outdoor field sports but also require fast film and lenses, after the fashion of the last category. You may care to consider black-and-white film, as it causes no problems with the colour of light sources and can be 'pushed' to very high speeds – effective ASA ratings as high as 1600 or even 3200 are quite possible.

HUNTING, SHOOTING, AND FISHING

Apart from the obvious dangers of doing anything in the company of guns, these can provide some excellent pictures; the actual progress of the hunt is rather like other horsey events, described below, but the initial gathering is relatively static and extremely colourful.

Shooting can concentrate on the guns, the dogs, the landscape, or even the bag; this is, after all, a traditional subject for a still life. Fishing usually concentrates on the peacefulness of the waiting, though the excitement of landing a game fish or the grace of fly-casting can also make good pictures. Game-fishing, on board a boat, is one of the few cases where a wide-angle lens is a positive advantage.

EQUESTRIAN EVENTS

This covers a vast range, from point-to-point to dressage to rodeos to racing. You will need a fairly close vantage point, but not as close as you might think: horses are <u>big</u>, and it is not too good an idea to stand where they might land on you. Amateur events are best, as you can get in among the action: racing is worst, and a long-focus lens is virtually essential.

Rather than wandering about, which endangers both you and the competitors, pick a good position – by a water-jump, for example, though you will need to beware of splashes – and stay there until there is a break in the action, when you may move elsewhere. At some amateur events, you can get an excellent position (if a trifle monotonous) by volunteering to act as a jump steward, replacing the poles knocked off in bad jumps.

At rodeos, try to get a place near the trap: otherwise, you will run into the usual problems associated with wide-ranging field events. The anticipation and apprehension on the rider's face is usually well worth recording.

MOTOR RACING, CYCLE RACING, AIR SHOWS

These fall firmly into two categories – those where you can get in among it, and those where you are stuck at a considerable distance. Most professional motor races, motor cycle races, and air days are in this latter category: the very worst are powerboat races, where there is very rarely any chance of getting close enough to use a standard lens.

In these cases, the best thing to do is to concentrate on the preparations, the aircraft on the ground, and the pits – and, of course, the spectators. It is just not worth trying to photograph a motor race or the like from a distance, and aircraft are even worse; you get a few flecks in an otherwise featureless sky, made worse by the fact that exposure is extremely difficult and you have a choice of sky detail and silhouetted airplanes, or airplane detail (such as can be seen on that scale) and a washed-out sky.

Some events, though, allow you to get frighteningly close. Typical examples are motorcycle scrambles, four-wheel-drive events, and rallies. The only limitation is your personal attitude towards your safety and that of the competitors, and you can get some superb pictures with a standard lens. Surprisingly enough, even top-class cycle races are often very sparsely attended, and you can get very good pictures of big-name riders.

OUTDOOR ATHLETICS

Once again, local events are much easier to photograph than international ones – and although world records may not be set, the opportunities for pictures are no less.

The track (running) events can be covered three ways: the start (essentially a static subject!), the race itself (with panning a

Praktica B200. 35mm single lens reflex, f1.8 50mm interchangeable bayonet mount lens, aperture priority automatic exposure, manual override, shutter 1/40-1/1000, delayed action.

The most effective sports *pictures are those that capture a sense of excitement, and subsequently convey this feeling to the viewer. The pictures may be of a single moment of daring, as in the death-defying leap of a ski-jumper shown* **facing page right,** *or you may wish to show a sport or event, perhaps man's battle against nature as in a yacht race,* **above left and facing page left.** *Alternatively, you could concentrate on the skills of a single individual as in the picture of the white water canoeist* **top.** *Your approach should depend on personal preference; you are the viewer whom the pictures should excite, and only you can decide how this should be achieved.*

ACTION PHOTOGRAPHY

Cosmic Symbol. 35mm compact camera, f3.5 33mm lens, symbol focusing, manual exposure, shutter 1/15-1/250.

useful technique), and the finish, which is usually pretty dramatic. Pre-focus on a point three or four feet <u>after</u> the finishing tape for the best effects.

Field events are much more static, and the only problem is staying out of the way of flying projectiles. Come in as close as you can without getting in the way of the competitors for exciting pictures of facial expressions. With jumps, concentrate on three things: the take off, the 'dead point' (described earlier), and the landing: the actual run-up is usually hard to capture and in any case not very interesting.

CIRCUSES

These are usually surprisingly well lit, and are well within the capabilities of an f/2.8 lens and fast film. You will need a ringside seat for the best pictures, of course, and you may not have much success with the trapeze artists – the black background may fool both the meter in your camera and the meter in the automatic printing machines.

Flash is usually banned, and for good reason: it upsets the animals and can cause dangerous temporary blind spots in the performers' eyes – particularly serious with acrobats, high-wire acts, and trapeze artists.

THEATRE

Many theatres ban photography altogether during performances, and almost all ban flash – it upsets other patrons. You will need a fast (400 ASA) film, but an f/2.8 lens should be sufficient, and the best time to take pictures is at the dress rehearsal – a surprising number of theatres will let you in for this if you ask politely and tell them that you want to take photographs. Even at dress rehearsals, though, flash may upset the actors.

A further advantage of dress rehearsals is that you are free to stand up and move around – something which would make you very unpopular during a performance, and which would probably result in your being asked to leave.

OTHER OCCASIONS

Swimming galas, rowing, darts competitions, billiards, fairgrounds – the list of possible action subjects is endless. From the information given above, you should be able to work out some strategem for taking pictures. The important thing is to <u>try it</u>. Take a few frames – three or four pictures, maybe – in the conditions in question. When you get them back, take a good look at them – where you went wrong, and where you succeeded. In some cases, such as gross underexposure when you were already working at the limits of your camera's abilities, you cannot do very much (except buy another camera!) but surprisingly often, you will get an image – and it costs very little to find out.

Frozen movement in sports or action pictures can often appear rather static and lifeless, whereas blur can psychologically reinforce an impression of speed. The technique normally used to achieve this is panning, which, whilst it requires a certain degree of practice, can lead to exceptional results when mastered. Generally, it will show the subject in sharp relief whilst imparting a rushing blur *to the background. A slow shutter speed is selected and the moving object followed through the viewfinder before, during and after exposure. Cameras with a separate viewfinder are ideal, since the view is not interrupted by a mirror as in a single lens reflex camera. Separate sports or action finders can be fitted to the latter to overcome this problem.*

EVERYDAY LIFE

All the subjects we have talked about photographing so far have been events out of the ordinary – perhaps only slightly out of the ordinary, like a day in the country, or a Thanksgiving dinner, but still not the stuff of everyday life.

And yet, it is the details of everyday life which most affect us when we consider the past. "Ah yes," we say, "We had just got married and we were desperately poor . . . I was working for so-and-so's, with that idiot of a boss . . . what was his name, now?" Things which seemed perfectly ordinary at the time have a certain fascination a few years later. How many of the houses you have lived in have you photographed? How many of the cars you have owned? How many of the firms you have worked for, how many bosses, how many girlfriends? How many of the pubs you have drunk in, of the schools you have been to, of the friends you went out with?

Some of the details are tiny. When I was a boy, we almost invariably used to have ice cream and custard after Sunday dinner – an unusual delicacy, and one I have not had for many years. It would be quite amusing to have a picture of the whole family tucking into such a pudding! Others are of more general application: the change from the old pounds, shillings, and pence to decimal currency happened when I was at university: I wish I had photographed the local market, with the prices in the old money.

Minox 35 GT. 35mm compact camera, f2.8 35mm lens, scale focusing, aperture priority automatic exposure, shutter 30-1/500, delayed action.

Moving outwards from the purely personal memories, there are the buildings which have been torn down to make way for the new. I spent much of my childhood in Plymouth, which was more thoroughly altered, at least in the very centre, than any city in England by World War Two bombing. What the bombers did not complete, the city planners have: and although I thought I would never forget Drake's Circus the way it was, or Union Street, I find that the memories are not as clearly detailed as I would like them to be. The whole field of local archiving is quite fascinating, especially if undertaken as a long-term project with 'before' and 'after' pictures.

Although the whole idea of taking pictures for posterity may seem pretentious, that too is worth considering. Although mile upon mile of film is exposed every year, a very great deal of it will tell future generations next to nothing about the way that we lived. After all, a pretty girl in a swimsuit on the beach looks very much the same from one decade to another, though the fashion in swimsuits may change. But a street full of motor cars – well, just compare a picture from the 1950s with one taken recently. The cars, the shops, the fashions, the styles of signwriting and display – everything is different, even if the actual buildings and even the shop names are the same.

If the pictures had personal relevance, it would be even more interesting. In our family albums, there are pictures of my

Facing page. Left: The milling crowds and bright signs of a narrow Hong Kong street are suggestive of the industry and prosperity of a crowded island whose very existence depends on trade. Above: Balinese women and children bear gifts of fresh fruit as offerings to the spirits of their departed relatives. Remaining pictures: Streetmarkets, wherever they may be, always have plenty of colour both in the wares that are on display and the people who work there. If you are looking for such shots, an early morning outing is advisable as stalls will still be well stocked with produce and crowds thin enough to give you camera room. Compact 35mm cameras with their wide angle lenses are ideal for such candid character snaps.

EVERYDAY LIFE

father with his Rudge motorcycle; but I do not think that there is a single picture of him all kitted up for riding it on a cold day. There are no pictures of the interior of his house, of his old Ford which he bought when he and my mother were married, of the ships he sailed on – because all these things were everyday occurences, and not worth recording. Since I have been a keen photographer from the age of sixteen, my own life is more thoroughly documented; but I still have no pictures of the first girl I really fell for, or of the interior of my flat when I was at university, or of the majority of the cars that I have owned.

If you are serious about taking pictures for later generations, then colour print film is not really good enough. As described earlier, it will fade and discolour. But if you keep the negatives, it will be perfectly possible to make black and white prints from them for a hundred years or more; and with advances in technology, doubtless films (and prints) will become longer lived and methods of restoring faded images will improve.

DOMESTIC SCENES

Using flash, or fast film, try photographing a typical day at home: getting up, cooking and eating breakfast – even the interior of the bathroom! – getting off to work, returning in the evening. What sort of things do you do in the evenings? Watching television, reading books, playing games, sitting around talking to friends – you can photograph any of these.

Photograph the children, asleep, doing their homework, dressed in their school clothes, dressed in play clothes, dressed in fashionable clothes.

Photograph the various rooms in the house: think back to the first television you ever saw, and compare it to the one you watch now. Photograph the store cupboard – in twenty years

time, half the things there (or at least their labels and packaging) will appear quaint and old-fashioned. Photograph the garden, your car – everything!

AT WORK

Provided you do not waste too much time, or get in anyone's way too much, few firms will object to your taking photographs at work. Of course, there may be some sensitive areas such as the drawing office or prototype workshop, and in the services there will be still more restrictions, but a record of the place that you work in and the people with whom you worked will be a valuable personal record even if there is nothing particularly interesting about what you do. If, of course, you work in some rapidly changing, or even dying, industry then pictures a mere ten or fifteen years old would be fascinating. Think of the size of computers a few years ago: what fits on a desk top now, and costs a few thousand pounds, would have cost millions then and filled a whole air-conditioned room or even a suite of rooms.

Depending on your own status, and the general attitude of the firm, you may well find it advisable to seek permission from your immediate superior; if he is not too keen, then (subject to the politics of the situation) you may care to ask <u>his</u> superior; I have always found that if you go high enough, you will eventually find someone who will either give the project an enthusiastic go-ahead or provide a convincing reason (such as security) why it should not be done.

If the pictures are good enough, there is always the possibility that the editor of the house magazine would like to use them. Speaking as an ex-editor of such magazines, I can assure you that if your pictures are even half-way usable they will be used; getting pictures is one of the most difficult parts of

The changing seasons bring with them a different look to familiar scenes. Light, shade and colour alter daily before our very eyes, yet in a way so subtle that we often remain unaware of this gradual passage of time or its effect on our surroundings. Artists and poets, with their keener eyes, look to these changes for their inspiration, yet as a snapshotter, you too require a certain degree of alertness if photography is to remain enjoyable and the results freshly pleasing. Autumn's mellow golden colours and the skeletal shapes of the denuded trees, the youthful riot of Spring colour, the sleeping calm of Winter's white countryside or the bright rich green of Summer; all these can be used as themes in themselves, or simply as backdrops for other snaps that you may envisage. Beware of casting your own shadow into the picture area as shown **facing page, bottom.**

Keystone Everflash XR 408. 110 cartridge load pocket camera, f8 23mm lens, fixed focus, automatic exposure, shutter speed 1/125, built-in electronic flash.

EVERYDAY LIFE

producing such a magazine. It is unlikely to do your career any harm, either, if you are known as something of a live wire – always provided, of course, that you do not overstep the mark and become known instead as an infernal nuisance!

AT PLAY

We have already touched upon this in the previous chapter, but it is worth taking pictures even of an ordinary night down at the pub, of an everyday game of football (every Saturday, anyway), perhaps of a meal at a restaurant.

It is important, though, not to offend other people by taking the pictures. For example, it is the height of inconsiderate behaviour to fire a flashgun in a quiet restaurant where, perhaps, there are couples trying to pass a romantic evening. In such circumstances, if you cannot take the picture unobtrusively it is better not to take it at all. Depending on the sort of pubs you drink in, you may also find a certain amount of resistance even if you do not use flash: it is generally as well to have some story ready, about how you are trying to document your everyday life. If you are sincere, you will probably get the other person

interested; you may even end up with a better set of pictures, perhaps a new friend, as a result of this.

There are off-beat pictures you can take, too: pictures of the cinema queue, or of people playing pub games.

YOUR SURROUNDINGS

Apart from the buildings and the shops already mentioned, there is a lot more that makes up the city or town that you live in. There are the newspaper sellers, the shoe-shine boys (now almost extinct in England), the hot-chestnut sellers, the buskers, the tramps, the hot-gospellers, the boys and girls out parading to see and be seen. There are the soap box orators, some of whom get very nervous if you photograph them (I ask them sweetly if they are ashamed of what they are doing). There are the old men who sit on benches, reading their newspapers and smoking their pipes. There are local buses, taxis, policemen – all the things, in fact, which you would call 'local colour' if you were abroad. In a sense, though, you are in a different country: a different country from the past and the future, and a country which you can never revisit.

Kodak Instamatic 177X. 126 cartridge load,
f11 Kodar lens, fixed focus,
weather symbol exposure setting, shutter 1/40 and 1/80.

It has previously been said *that when photographing people, you should aim for close-ups to get the best effect. The pictures on the **facing page** however, show the type of meaningful shot that can be taken when thoughtfully reversing this principle. Suggestions as to composition should not be taken as rigid rules but rather as flexible guidelines. The pictures on these pages demonstrate the effect that ultra violet light can have on snow scenes on a clear sunny day. Whilst this blue cast is generally acceptable in snapshots, it can be reduced readily by fitting a skylight filter to your lens. Any remaining blue will add to the cold feel of the scene.*

MOVING ON

If you are happy with the results that you are getting, there is no reason ever to move on from the equipment which you are currently using. It may be, however, that you feel that you are limited by your equipment and that by buying a more versatile camera you could increase both the range of conditions under which you could take pictures and your success rate.

Before doing so, it is worth analysing your motives carefully. If you are merely succumbing to advertising pressure, or buying a fancy camera because it is the done thing, you may find that the decision is counterproductive; if photography becomes a big production, instead of a casual pleasure, you may find yourself leaving the camera at home and taking <u>fewer</u> pictures than before. If, on the other hand, you find that you are frustrated by not being able to control depth of field, action stopping, etc., creatively, it is worth considering buying a new camera.

For a variety of reasons, the most popular camera today is the 35mm single lens reflex, with the choice of automatic exposure or manual control. Whilst you are still getting used to it, you can rely on the exposure automation, but as you get more confident and skilled, you can start to override it more and more: eventually you may find that you hardly ever use the automation, though most people would admit that it is still very handy for snapshots.

Not only is the 35mm SLR relatively cheap to buy (largely because of its popularity, and versatility) and run (35mm film is very cheap per exposure – especially when the quality attainable is taken into consideration); it is also easy to focus, and is free from parallax error; it accepts a wide range of interchangeable lenses and other accessories, and it strikes a good balance between handiness and image quality.

The make of camera you buy is not particularly important, except that you tend to get what you pay for. The very cheapest cameras should be avoided, because they cut so many corners in order to economise: optical quality may be disappointing, features are lacking, handling may be awkward, and mechanical finish and reliability may not be very impressive. On the other hand, a number of top-flight manufacturers provide an entry-level auto-only SLR at a very reasonable price. The Nikon EM, for example, is less than a third of the price of the top-of-the-line F3, but it shares the same lens mount and is a part of the same system.

Whilst choosing a camera must be a personal matter, as a camera may be the best-made and most versatile in the world but still uncomfortable in the hands, it is worth remembering that you may want to change or upgrade your equipment still further at a later date, and that some manufacturers have a very much better record of continuity than others.

Apart from the basic camera, there are the extra lenses and accessories – and indeed, unless you take advantage of these, there is little point in buying a 'system' camera.

The most obvious accessories are of course the lenses, and the larger manufacturers offer an amazing array. Nikon offer several dozen, ranging from a fish-eye which covers an angle of 220° (and thus actually 'seeing' <u>behind</u> the photographer) through wide-angles to standard lenses and on to a 2000mm telephoto which covers an angle of $1\frac{1}{4}$° enough for a head-and-shoulders portrait at sixty feet.

Neither extreme is much use to the average amateur (or even the average professional), and the 20mm-200mm range fulfils most people's needs – though devotees of bird photography, or motor racing, may well use 300mm, 500mm, or even longer lenses.

Before buying any extra lenses, consider why you want them. Are you always trying to get more in than the standard lens

Olympus XA-2. 35mm compact camera,
f3.5 35mm lens, symbol focusing,
automatic programmed exposure, shutter 2-1/750,
delayed action, accepts dedicated flash.

*Facing page. Top: A picture
frame sets off a photograph, and
similarly a subject within a
snap can be "framed." Here, the
window of a New York cab
draws full attention to the
driver. Such effects can be either
found or contrived, but they are
invariably effective. **Bottom:**
When photographing the
interaction of two people, show
both figures. The reason for the
girl's joy would have been lost
had she alone been rendered in*

*close-up. © Walt Disney
Productions. A wide variety of
objects shown in sharp focus,
whilst frequently distracting,
can sometimes give interest and
meaning to a snap. **Left:**
Baskets are obviously important
to this woman's livelihood. **Top
and above:** A carefully chosen
prop can convey a great deal of
information in such posed,
portrait type shots. Guns and a
shepherd's crook leave no doubt
as to the interests of the figures
in these pictures.*

MOVING ON

can manage? If so, consider a wide angle. The popular 35mm focal length is comparatively cheap and provides image quality comparable with the standard lens whilst covering about twice the area at any given distance. Many people consider that it is too close to the standard lens, though, and go for a 28mm instead: this covers about three times the area, although the perspective can begin to look a little strange. Others go for 24mm, which covers four times the area, and the 20mm lens covers over six times the area shown by the standard lens, but gives some quite odd distortion effects.

If, on the other hand, you are trying to pick out details the whole time, you may need a longer lens (or, of course, you may be able to move in closer). Although 135mm is the traditional first choice a lens of something like 85mm, 90mm, or 105mm, is much better for portraiture and picking out nearby details, whereas a 200mm or longer can really pull in distant detail.

Zoom lenses are an attractive option in some ways, but the trouble is that most people ask too much of them. They want a long zoom range (say the 3:1 of a 70-210mm), a fast maximum aperture (though f/3.5 is pretty fast for a zoom – they seldom approach fixed-length lenses in this respect), light weight, low cost, and (preferably) close or 'macro' focusing as well. To meet any one of those requirements is difficult and expensive; to meet any two of them is about the limit of modern optical science; and to combine any three is effectively impossible. Settle for a more modest specification, and the results will be very much better.

You may also wish to consider a really fast lens if you habitually take pictures in poor lighting; a 'macro' lens, designed to provide superb image quality even when focused down to a few inches (and with a focusing mount which permits this); extension tubes, or bellows, which allow you to focus your existing lenses still closer; and teleconverters which fit between your existing lenses and the camera, doubling or even trebling the focal length (so that a 50mm becomes a 100mm or 150mm) at the expense of reduced aperture (f/2 becomes f/4 or f/5.6) and reduced image quality – but they are cheap and compact, and many professionals own one as a method of 'getting out of trouble' when they need a longer lens than they have with them.

Of the other accessories, a motor drive or autowinder is almost invariably unnecessary, and uses film at an alarming rate, but is great fun: a tripod is very useful for supporting long lenses; filters can be used to 'correct' the response of the film so that it more closely corresponds to what you see, or for special effects; a cable release stops you jarring the camera when it is held on a tripod; and a gadget bag helps you carry it all about.

You may wish to consider breaking away from 35mm and using rollfilm. Because of the bigger negative, a rollfilm camera will always outperform a 35mm camera of equal quality in terms of image quality. Twin-lens reflexes give superb pictures at very low cost, but for maximum versatility a rollfilm reflex is best. These are very expensive, but they are a staple of professional usage.

The Minox sub-miniature is smaller than the smallest 110, and takes a tiny 8 x 11mm negative on special film. The results are surprisingly good, and the camera is very small and easy to carry: but processing is expensive. The Pentax and Minolta 110 SLRs are fun, but the saving in size does not really warrant the drop in quality.

You may also wish to consider doing your own darkroom work. Whilst there is no point in doing this if you use colour slide (where you have very little control over the process anyway), if you want the finest prints there is little doubt that the best way to get them is to do them yourself, whether in colour or black-and-white.

Minolta Hi-matic AF2. 35mm compact camera,
f2.8 38mm lens, automatic focusing,
automatic programmed exposure, shutter 1/8-1/430,
built-in electronic flash.

Processing films is a fairly simple mechanical process, requiring only the ability to follow instructions: many photographers process their own black and white (because it is cheap and easy, you can influence the quality of the final negative, and anyway force of habit is behind them), but have colour film – both slide and negative – trade processed by a professional laboratory.

Printing is, at its lowest level, no more difficult than film processing, but as you get more practised and grow more critical it becomes less and less mechanical and becomes more and more an art; there is a great pleasure in coaxing the best out of a negative, so that the final print is something to be proud of.

And this is the essential beauty of photography: it is an immensely rich and versatile medium, capable of being manipulated to an almost unbelievable extent to reflect your own personal vision. You never stop learning, either about photography or about what you photograph. You are constantly made more aware of everything, more alive; and unless you are very determined indeed, you are freed from mere practicality and allowed into the realms of beauty.

Wherever you may live or travel, street life is always a vibrant, colourful and ever changing source of snapshots. It may be that you are part of this life, in which case the pictures will hold a personal significance, or it may be that you are simply the interested and inquisitive outsider. If the latter applies, some scenes may need a tactful, even covert approach if the feelings of others are to be considered.

ACKNOWLEDGEMENTS

The publishers would like to express their
grateful thanks for technical information
and for the loan of equipment to:

Dixons Photographic Limited.
Photopia Limited.
Technical and Optical Equipment (London) Limited.
Keystone Cameras (UK) Limited.
Konishiroku UK.
J. Osawa and Company (UK) Limited.
E. Leitz (Instruments) Limited.
Nikon (UK) Limited.
Polaroid (UK) Limited.
Kodak Limited.
Olympus Optical Company (UK) Limited.
Hanimex (UK) Limited.
Vivitar (UK) Limited.
Photax Limited.
Minolta (UK) Limited.
C.Z. Scientific Instruments (Elstree) Limited.

First published in Great Britain 1982 by Colour Library International Ltd.
© 1982 Illustrations and text: Colour Library International Ltd., New Malden, Surrey, England.
Colour separations by LA CROMOLITO, Milan, Italy.
Display and text filmsetting by Acesetters Ltd., Richmond, Surrey, England.
Printed and bound in Barcelona, Spain by JISA-RIEUSSET & EUROBINDER.
All rights reserved.
ISBN 0 86283 009 5
COLOUR LIBRARY INTERNATIONAL